The Standard-bred Cornish Fowl; a Practical
Treatise on Their Standard Requirements--
mating and Breeding--rearing--housing--
training and Conditioning for Exhibition--
judging and Utility Values--genetics and
Mendelism Outlined, Etc.

03477-36　00-0189

94   3   F-13/4

THE CORNISH FOWL

A History of the Breed and Its Development in America

FRED. H. BOHRER

THE $|\mathcal{W}$

STANDARD-BRED
CORNISH FOWL

A PRACTICAL TREATISE ON THEIR STANDARD REQUIREMENTS—
MATING AND BREEDING—REARING—HOUSING—TRAINING
AND CONDITIONING FOR EXHIBITION—JUDGING
AND UTILITY VALUES—GENETICS AND
MENDELISM OUTLINED, ETC.

by

FRED H. BOHRER

Secretary-Treasurer of the American Cornish Club, Editor of the American Cornish
Club Annual Year-book and the Club Publication, "THE CORNISH
CHRONICLE", Official Club Judge, Registered Judge
of the American Poultry Association, Judge
and Official Registrar of the National
Breeders' and Fanciers'
Association

ILLUSTRATED

The AMERICAN STANDARD OF PERFECTION is used as a basis
of the Text and Illustrations

UTICA, NEW YORK
1922

SF489
.C6B6

no 1

A CONTRAST

How the Cornish fowl differs in physical make-up from the loose-feathered breeds.

*   ### PREFACE
                      —

My viewpoint of Cornish may be slightly different from that of some present-day fanicers, on account of long association with the breed and the fact that I watched it emerge from a mass of nondescript fighting fowls bred originally for pit use in natural spurs, and for that purpose first brought to America.

Many kinds of grade Orientals—some English-made crosses, others of pure East Indian blood—were bred in England as " Indian Game " when the first club was organized and an effort made to establish certain features and colors as the proper thing for exhibition purposes. The winning birds of those days were not extremely large. Some cocks as light as eight pounds and few over ten. Then in the early '90's came a rage for longer legs and greater weight, and an apparent mixing on the otherside with some soft-feathered race. This was found to be a mistake and later there came an infusion of more Aseel blood, a reversion to the Oriental in type with the low blocky " battleship " form. This return to the Aseel which was advocated and pursued by myself in America before it was taken up by the fanciers of Britain, produced the Cornish of to-day. My only fear now is that our British friends may go too far. They often incline toward extremes. Let us stop at the Aseel type. Do not encourage blockiness to the extent of turning the Cornish into a Dorking.

Another point: If we follow our slogan " Cornish on Every Farm," we must produce such Cornish as will be able to take care of themselves on a farm. Not the listless waddling fourteen pounder, but a bird of some sprightliness and ability to hustle. One that can go after a grasshopper and catch him. It seems to me that present Standard weights are better than heavier ones would be, both for the egg basket and also for the general popularity of the fowl. Even in a " beef breed," quality should be considered before quantity.

There has long been a need for a real breed book on Cornish. Those old monographs of the early days, by Whitfield and Babcock, were written at a time when the fowl was still in a developing stage, and as a consequence, the books became out of date within a very few years after their publication. I started a similar work myself in 1893 but never completed it. The preliminary chapters were printed in the " Game Fowl Monthly." Since that time nothing has been done until our worthy Club Secretary, Mr. Bohrer, was finally persuaded to get busy with his pen. Now at last we have an up-to-date treatise that does justice to our breed. It should be appreciated by fanciers, and will help teach the general public how fascinating and valuable Cornish really are. May this little volume meet with the success it truly deserves.'

[Signed]   H. P. CLARKE.
Indianapolis, Ind.

INTRODUCTION

The Cornish fowl in America came from England. The Cornish or Indian Game fowl in England has a vague origin. The history of ages is behind it. The glamor of antiquity envelopes it, making it inseparable from the history of nations long since dead. Its forebears rambled and fought in the palaces of kings and the courts of princes, and were bartered for wives in the market places.

On account of the increasing popularity of the breed in America, and its established position among the fancy and utility fowls of Great Britain, this book has been written to help spread the knowledge of its merits. An attempt has been made to touch on all phases of raising Cornish.

An exhaustive study has been made of Cornish history and of methods of breeding both past and present, with a view to giving the reader a comprehensive knowledge of the breed, in one volume. Many avenues of information have been searched. No effort has been spared to obtain the most accurate data. The varieties of American origin, the White, Buff and White Laced Red Cornish, have much to commend them to the beginner, and the most accurate information obtainable has been given.

The writer is indebted for much of the history of the breed and for the cuts to Dr. H. P. Clarke, Indianapolis; Dr. J. Leslie Davis, Philadelphia, Pa.; Chas. S. Brent, Oconomowoc, Wis.; W. S. Templeton, Santa Clara, Cal.; W. H Card, Manchester, Conn., and Courtland H. Smith, Warrenton, Va.; also to excerpts from the year books of the American Cornish Club, "The Cornish Chronicle," "The Poultry Item," "The Reliable Poultry Journal," and "Everybody's Poultry Magazine."

Grateful acknowledgment is made to my brother, Dr. J. William Bohrer, New York City, for reading and suggesting revisions in copy and proofs.

The CORNISH FOWL is sent forth on its journey with the sincere hope that it may prove an inspiration and help to all who are interested in poultry breeding, whether Cornish or any other breed of poultry.

FRED H. BOHRER.

Utica, N. Y.

The Standard-bred Cornish Fowls

CHAPTER I

ORIGIN AND HISTORY

The Genealogy—In attempting to establish the genealogy of the Cornish fowl, it is necessary, first, to trace through antiquity the influence of the Aseel fowl of India on the breed. The word " aseel " (1) is derived from the Arabic asil, meaning "noble," and not, as is usually supposed, from the asl, meaning " thorough-bred." The name being common in Indian, it is not surprising to learn that the first mention of this historic fowl is to be found in the Code of Manu, a post-Buddist group of laws, written some three hundred years before Christ, wherein cock fighting was established as a popular sport. The Aseel fowl is occasionally referred to in later parchments which state that it is indigenous to the country about Agra, Delhi and Lucknow, India. Mention has been made that the breed abounded in the garden of Gethsemane. During the rule of the Caesars, this fowl was most commonly used for fighting and bartering. We have little exact data of its early history, most of what is known about the Aseel fowl of olden days coming to us principally from books of travel, or from log-books of tramp sailing vessels.

Cock fighting is one of the oldest pastimes known to man. The Aseel fowl, due to its pugnacity, has become a heritage from the ancient world. Much mystery and romanticism is shrouded about the breed. Few countries can be excluded from the list of breeders of the fighting cock. As travel became more common, and conquests of rising empires' spread, it is natural to suppose that soldiers, invading different lands, had with them their pet fighting cocks. Thus, the early existence of the Aseel fowl in England was due to Roman gladiators; this would solve the mystery of its presence there at the time of the Druids.

The Fowls of the Orient—The Aseel fowl has stamped its type on its progeny so firmly that it may be stated that there is little difference between the ancient syecimens and those found in England before breeding and crossing became of any importance. They have been much the same at all times. Exceptions have been noted. The so-called " cullum " breed of India is a mongrel type of Aseel, kept by the natives for " naked-heel "

1—F. G Duttan first applied the name Aseel to the breed in England about 1875.

fighting. Then there is the type known as the Kadir cock, like the Aseel found in the southern part of India; also the Bhenghums, with single combs, which vary little from the original Aseel; and the Chittagong, a long-legged fowl of little game tendencies.

The Cornish fowl as a distinct breed never existed in India. The name Cornish was brought into use prior to 1886 in connec-

CORNISH ANCESTORS

Representing the type coming from India known as "Pheasant Malay" or "Indian Game."

tion with and to distinguish from fowls of the Aseel type and the original Indian Game,* and was quoted in the "Fanciers' Gazette" (London) in the issue of April 16, 1886, by Mr. George Payne, originator of Pyle and Duckwing Leghorns. The Aseel fowl of India may be called the direct parent to Cornish and Malay, grandparent to the Brahma, and patriarch to all peacomb varieties, except the Sumatra.

*—The term "Indian Game" is now obsolete in connection with the Cornish fowl. No mention of the Indian Game is made in the A. P. A. Standard of Perfection.

The Standard of the 19th Century—In Europe, up to the 19th Century, the standard of the Aseel fowl was very low and indefinite. There was no classification of the breed, either of the pure blooded stock or of Aseel crosses. Poultry literature yields very little information. Etchings and paintings known to have been made after the Renaissance, which began in Italy in the 14th Century and gradually spread over western Europe, show the Aseel and the Black-Breasted Malays as typical barnyard fowl.

Concerning the situation prior to the establishment of the Indian Game Club in England in 1886, Dr. H. P. Clarke, pioneer authority on Game breeds in America, in an article written for the " Inland Poultry Journal," July, 1908, states that an examination of the show reports in the two leading English poultry periodicals, "The Live Stock Journal" and the "Fanciers' Gazette," reveals that at Bath in 1887 a genuine " Indian Game," was exhibited in the A. O. V.* class. This was the first time, he states, that the name ever occurred in any poultry publication.

The Name " Indian Game "—Dr. Clarke evidently believes that the classes were filled with a hodge-podge of sizes and colors, Aseels pure and grade, Pheasant Malays, Old English Game crosses, and every imaginable combination of the three; also, that the name " Indian Game " represented a group rather than a single breed or variety, and covered all Oriental fowls excepting the Malays. Mention is made of Tegetmeier's old " Poultry Book " (1856) and Wright's " Book of Poultry," apparently written about 1887, in neither of which is an attempt made to distinguish among the Indian Game, Cornish and the Aseel.

It is evident that there must have been a sudden change, a radical revision, of the standard of the three examples of the Indian importation and the native English crosses. The highest flight in the fancy of the transmutationists certainly could not have changed the characteristics of these closely similar breeds. It is believed that such change was only possible through the growth of scientific experiments, and the attempt of the breeders to try new combinations in mating.

What Authorities Believe—G. T. Whitfield, of England, in his discussion, " Origin of the Indian Game," believes that the origin of the " Indian Game " can only be guessed at. The fowl as it existed in England, he states, was an improvement on the Indian importations, having been crossed with the Malay.

One of the more widely accepted views concerning the early origin of the Cornish is given expression by a Mr. Montressor in " Poultry." He states that the Aseel differs from the Cornish in that the letter is purely of English birth. He claims that he was given personal information in 1846 by the late Sir Walter Raleigh Gilbert, who imported from India some red Aseels into Cornwall, and there crossed them with the Derby Black Reds.

---

*—Term used to designate class of fowls of no recognized standard. The initials stand for Any Old Variety.

and later the Sumatra Game.* Sir William Call gets similar credit for having introduced into England, in the early '40's of the last century, the fowl known as the " Indian Game."

Following the history from 1846 to 1870, when it has been stated birds showing an element of Malay blood were shown in a fine and numerous class at the Plymouth (England) show,

HYDERABAD GAME

An old R. P. J. sketch representing the type of Cornish in England and America about 1888.

Cornish may be said to have been improved by the introduction of Black Indian Game blood. Larger specimens were produced and the male birds had solid black breasts as a result.

Conforming to a Standard—After the heterogenous elements of the Aseel-Malay-Mongrel-Indian Game combination had been sorted out, worked over, and made to conform to a standard, it may be stated that the fowl classed as Cornish then obtained recognition as a distinct breed.

Dr. Clarke, in an article in the " Poultry Monthly," June, 1901, entitled, " Origin and History," mentions an account of a most successful prize-winning bird in the west of England which was the offspring of a Pheasant-Malay cock and a common barnyard hen. He also mentions Cornish that were descended from Indian mongrels, Malay, Langshan and British Game, and goes on record with the statement that the Cornish fowl of to-day is neither a pure breed nor the direct result of any particular cross or combination, but rather the intermingling of several, in which the markings (though not necessarily the blood) of the old Pheas-

---

*—No trace of the Sumatra Game could be found in Britain until 1902. Edward Brown's " Races of Domestic Poultry."

ant Malay and the laced Aseel predominate. And again, Dr. Clarke reiterates in the "American Fancier," July, 1901, that Cornish are nothing more than "grade Aseel." He compares the expression to that of a "grade Jersey," which is not pure but contains just enough of the Jersey blood to make predominant the characteristics of this breed. He states that the Cornish fowl is strong in reproductive power, so much so, that from a mated Aseel cock and hen of any large sized, smooth legged variety, an offspring may be obtained from which the Cornish fowl may be easily evolved by a little selection in breeding. Dr Clarke claims to have produced typical Cornish without a particle of Cornish blood to start with, believing that it is not necessary to have a particular cross or mating, such as the Aseel-Derby cross, that Montressor mentions Sir Walter Raleigh Gilbert made. From the variation in style, carriage and disposition, much consideration must be given the Clarke theory of the origin of the Cornish.

Fixing a Birthday—To fix upon a birthday for the Cornish, it seems that it is necessary to do one of two things, viz.: start its career with the time when it first stood alone (about 1886), or begin its history with the pre-exhibition era, when the Cornish represented a group class rather than an individual one, when the old Pheasant Malay represented the nearest approach to a distinct variety of any of those breeds later merged into Cornish.

When the Indian Game Club organized at Plymouth, England, April 15, 1886, the Cornish variety was designated a definite type, and differentiated from other Oriental varieties and crosses grouped under the heading of "Indian Game." Following this meeting, John Harris, of Liskeard, Cornwall, unquestionably the highest English authority on Game fowls at that time, wrote an article to the "Fanciers' Gazette" (London) April 22, 1886, in which he stated that Malay and old fighting Game crosses were eligible for the "Indian Game" classes. And then in 1886 the first article describing this breed in America appeared in the April number of the "Game Fowl Monthly."

The First Standard—The first standard for Cornish was made by the Indian Game Club of England, December 1, 1886, and readopted in 1891. It was during the early period of the existence of this club that Cornish began to command attention in America. The "Poultry World" of June, 1887, was the first general poultry periodical in the United States to print an article on the Cornish fowl.

Importing Cornish—The importation of Cornish was the next step that followed. Dr. H. P. Clarke, of Indianapolis, Ind., is conceded to be the pioneer of this breed in America. In August, 1887 he imported Cornish "Indians" to Irvington, a suburb of Indianapolis. In the same month the "Game Fowl Monthly" published the first illustration of Cornish to appear in any poultry book or periodical in the world. Dr. Clarke exhibited the birds he had imported, at the Indiana State Fair, a month after he received them. A year later, in January, 1888, he exhibited them

again, this time at the National American Poultry Association
Show, held in Indianapolis, Ind. The second importation was a
setting of Cornish "Indian" eggs, made by H. S. Babcock, of
Providence, R. I., in December, 1887. Thus the implantation of
Cornish on American soil is fixed. Although there have been
some conflicting stories about the first importations in America,

AN OLD ENGLISH GAME COCK

No trace of the blood of this fowl is to be found in the
Cornish of to-day. This type of fowl was formerly used for
crossing to increase the speed in fighting.

time has erased the inaccurate data that blazed forth during the
" boom" of Cornish in the early '90's. For purposes of adver-
tising, there were a number of importers and breeders who claimed to have " bred Cornish exclusively the longest," and named
dates that went back to the late '70's and early '80's. A breeder
in Missouri took up Cornish in 1897, and it is known that he
never made a prior claim in print, but had others do it for him.
He gave to representatives of the " Reliable Poultry Journal," a
story of having imported in 1877 a trio of birds from England,
and furnished them with feathers claimed to have been received
at that time. Another also claimed to have been the oldest breeder
in America, giving a date of 1887. But the writer has been in-

formed that he received his birds from C. A. Sharp & Co., of Lockport, N. Y., the latter having purchased the pen of Cornish sent over in January, 1889, to the International Exhibition at Buffalo, N. Y., by G. T. Whitfield, of Market Drayton, England.

The Ohio " Poultry Journal " in 1888, printed a letter in the " Game Department," conducted by Dr. Clarke, from the famous old Cornishman, John Harris. It follows:

> " Cornish are neither Indian nor Game, but are made up of a cross between Game and Pheasant Malay and true Malay. I know all the history of this fraud and its promoters. One of the most successful exhibitors is my neighbor, and he claimed a cock at two guineas in the selling class at the West of England Show, which was bought by a man here from a farm yard at half a dollar. This bird was bred from a Malay cock and a common hen. They have formed a club for this so-called breed and published a standard of points, and as I know the whole crowd, I will take oath that not one of them ever bred a Cornish fowl in his life.
>
> " You may publish this if you like with my name. I don't think you Americans, with all your 'new breeds' ever did a bigger fizzle than this Cornish dodge.
>
> " Some time ago in ' Fanciers' Gazette' (England), I offered to give a cup if any of the members could produce a single bird which they had bred, and which Captain Astley (who was then in England and the acknowledged authority on Indian Game fowl) would identify as Indian Game. After this I need not say that English cockers are not such idiots as to use these birds in the pit."

This letter was no doubt incited by the frequent importations of birds by Americans, and the Cornish fowl boom which was beginning to sweep the country. The importers were principally Messrs. A. D. Arnold, Babcock, Bowman, Sharp and F. A. Webster, who, during the years of 1889 and 1890, received more English birds than has ever been equalled since.

American Clubs Organized—In February, 1890, at the New York Show, the American Indian Game Club was organized, and Mr. Babcock, of Providence, R. I., elected president, and Mr. O. K. Sharp, of Lockport, N. Y., secretary-treasurer. During that year 60 members were reported on the Club's roster.

About this time the merits of the Cornish fowl spread to the Pacific coast. John D. Mercer bought a trio of the breed from Mr. Babcock which he received in Los Angeles in 1890. The first setting of eggs reached Dr. Urmy, of Los Angeles soon after.

On January 11, 1892, a standard for Cornish was adopted at the annual club meeting in Philadelphia, Pa. In the same year, the Northwestern Indian Game Club was organized with the following officers: John D. Mercer, president; J. H. Rengsterff, vice president; Sidney W. Loeb, secretary-treasurer; W. H. Piling and

F. T. Palmer, organizing committee. In 1893, the name was changed to the Pacific Indian Game Club.

At the meeting of the American Poultry Association in 1893, Dark Cornish was admitted to the " American Standard of Perfection." Five years later, in 1898, White Cornish was admitted to the Standard.

The Early Struggle for Existence—There was a gradual decline in the popularity of the breed soon after the Pan-American Exposition at Buffalo, N. Y., in 1901. About that time the American Indian Game Club had a membership of 16, through whose efforts special prizes were offered at the Exposition.. After this the club gasped its last. The Cornish fowl declined in popularity steadily until 1906. Then a few enthusiastic fanciers tried to revive it. During the summer of 1907, Rev. H. A. Huey, of Michigan, secured a number of initiation fees, as an acting secretary. In January, 1908, a number of western fanciers, including Charles S. Brent, W. S. Templeton and F. H. Williams, with a few others showed birds at Chicago, Ill., determined to keep the breed in the public favor. W. S. Templeton succeeded in having the American Poultry Association transfer the membership of the old American Indian Game Club to the organization called the American Cornish Club in such a way that the A. C. C. appeared to be the reorganized successor. But in reality it was the same club with the same active members, with the addition of a few new breeders. The increase in membership from February, 1907, to January, 1908, was 14 to 75. On September 23, 1907, the Pacific Indian Game Club's name was changed to the Pacific Cornish Fowl Club. Renewed interest seems to have been provoked since the birth of the American Cornish Club.

Changing the Classes—The White Laced Red variety of Cornish was admitted by the American Poultry Association on August 12, 1909; and that organization four years later, in August, 1913, admitted all Cornish to the English class in the " American Standard of Perfection." There were members of the club not in full accord with the last ruling of the American Poultry Association. It occasioned much dissension; some thought that the fowl would become loose-feathered and should be placed permanently in the Oriental class, while others strongly favored the admission to the English class, in order to make the breed more popular. Whatever may have been the individual belief of some of the American breeders, the fact remains that so much publicity has been given Cornish since it has been placed permanently in the new class that few show secretaries now attempt to put it in any other than the English class.

The original Cornish in England contained very little Aseel blood. It seems to have been the aim of the British fanciers to breed out the Oriental type, and it was not until about 1900 that they returned to the original model adopted by the Americans. Therefore the classification of Cornish as English may suffice if its birth is dated by the organization of the Indian Game Club in England in 1886.

Many Members—Almost 600 members were listed in the American Cornish Club during the years of 1919 and 1920. This is the greatest number ever recorded in the history of any club specializing in Cornish, either in the United States or Great Britain.

In 1891, H. S. Babcock made the following prefatory remark in a monograph, " The Indian Game," which was prophetic in its substance. It stated, " At this time the facts concerning the earliest importations of the Indian Game into the United States are sufficiently fresh in the minds of breeders to enable them to be stated accurately, but with each succeeding year, these facts will grow more and more obscure, and in their places will appear myths more or less monstrous." This prophecy has been strikingly fulfilled.

CHAPTER II

THE STANDARD OF THE CORNISH BREED *

General Appearance—From a rear or upper view, the shoulders, wings and back should be bullock-heart shaped, while the profile view—the backbone, chest, keel and stern—should resemble the outline of an egg, the large end formost and uppermost, and the front point of the keel nearly on a level with the angle at the juncture of the back and tail.

Scale of Points

	Shape	Color	Total
Station	8	----	8
Beak	1	1	2
Head	3	1	4
Eyes	1	1	2
Comb	4	----	4
Wattles	1	----	1
Earlobes	1	1	2
Neck	4	3	7
Back	6	3	9
Breast	6	3	9
Keel	5	----	5
Body and Stern	4	3	7
Wings	4	3	7
Tail	4	3	7
Legs and Feet	6	4	10
Hardness of Feathers	4	----	4
Condition	----	----	6
Weight	----	----	6
Possible Points, Total			100

Standard Weights

Cocks, 9½ lbs.

Hens, 7 lbs.

Cockerels, 8 lbs.

Pullets, 6 lbs.

Weight Disqualification—All specimens more than three (3) pounds under standard weights are disqualified.

Shape of Male

Head—Short, deep and broad, the crown projecting over the eyes, which should be wide apart, indicating great vigor and strong constitution.

---

*—The A. P. A. Standard is copyrighted, its use in this book is prohibited. Prospective exhibitors should follow the "Standard of Perfection."

Beak—Short, well curved, thick, strong and stout, adding to the powerful appearance of the bird.

Eyes—Of good size, full, with bold and fearless expression, not sunken,
in the sense of being close together, though they may have a sunken appearance due to the overhanging brows and protruding cheeks.

Face—Slightly pebbly, strong in texture, dotted with small feathers.

PRE-STANDARD CORNISH TYPE

In the early days there was no definite Cornish type. These
representatives are more like the tall and rangy Malay type
rather than the low and blocky Aseel type.

Comb—Pea, small, distinct, free from twists, rather short, evenly arched,
low, firmly set upon broad strong base, well down at rear point.

Wattles and Earlobes—Wattles very scant, even, strong texture. Earlobes, small, strong in texture.

Neck—Medium in length, slightly arched; throat dotted with small
feathers; hackle, moderately short, just nicely covering base of neck.

Back—Medium in length; top line of back slightly convex, not sway-
back, free from any inclination toward bridging to tail; sloping downward
from base of neck to tail, and slightly sloping from each side of the backbone; well filled in at base of neck, the neck-cape being very broad and
full, and shoulder-capes wide apart; hip bones very wide apart and well
covered with muscles, but the saddle must not be dished; very broad across

the shoulders, carrying its width well back to a line with the thighs, show-ing good width between the wings, and then narrowing to the tail; saddle feathers, scant, short, and very tight fitting.

Breast—Very wide, very deep, well rounded at the sides, full projecting forward beyond wing-fronts when the specimen is standing erect; feathers short, tucked between wings at the sides.

Keel—Long, strong, free from crooks; well tucked up in stern, diverging from the back as it extends forward in a somewhat curved line, the front end well embedded in flesh, meeting a very full swelled chest.

Body and Stern—Body well rounded at sides; feathers short. Stern well tucked up; feathers scant, very short and tight fitting.

Wings—Short, very stout, powerful, closely folded; shoulders nearly level or slightly drooping to harmonize with slope of back; wing-fronts, standing out prominently from the body at the shoulders; wing points, some-what rounded but well converged at extreme ends when folded; closely tucked at ends and held about on a line with lower tails converts or slightly wider.

Tail—Short, compact, closely folded when the specimen is standing at ease, carried nearly horizontally, slightly drooping preferred; sickles and coverts very narrow.

Legs and Feet—Legs straight not more than slightly bent at hock joints when specimen is standing easily erect; thighs, of medium length, round, thick, stout, bulging with muscular development, set wide apart; shanks, short, well rounded, stout in bone, smoothly scaled, standing evenly and well apart   Feet, large, flat; toes, strong, rather thick, medium in length, straight, well spread, the hind toes set low and extending backward; nails, strong and well shaped.   Shanks, feet and toes, free from feathers and down.

Plumage—Short, narrow, hard, wiry, very glossy.

Body in hand—Firm, compact, very muscular.

Station, carriage and style—Station moderately low; carriage and style, very erect, upright, commanding, giving an appearance of great vigor, alert, graceful in movements.

Size—The specimen should be of sufficient size to possess standard weight in normal breeding condition.

Shape of Female

Head—Short, deep and broad, the crown projecting over the eyes which should be wide apart, indicating great vigor and strong constitution.

Beak—Short, well curved, thick, strong and stout, adding to the power-ful appearance of the bird.

Eyes—Of good size, full, with bold and fearless expression, not sunken, in the sense of being close together, though they may have a sunken appearance due to the overhanging brows and protruding cheeks.

Face—Slightly pebbly, strong in texture, dotted with small feathers.

Comb—Pea, very small, distinct, free from twists, rather short, evenly arched, low, firmly set upon broad, strong base, well down at rear point.

Wattles and Earlobes—Wattles, very scant, even, strong in texture. Earlobes, small, strong in texture.

Neck—Medium in length; top line of back slightly convex ,not swaybacked, free from any inclination toward a cushion or bridging to the tail; sloping downward from the base of the neck to the tail, and slightly sloping from each side of backbone; well filled in at base of neck, the neck-cape being very broad and full and shoulder capes wide apart; hip bones very wide apart and well covered with muscles, but the back must not be dished; very broad across the shoulders, carrying its width well back to a line with

A DARK CORNISH FEATHER

The black edge represents the lacing, the black center a stripe, the intermediate black a penciling, while the light portions represent the mahogany ground color.

the thighs, showing good width between wings, and then narrowing to the tail; the feathers are scant, short and very tight-fitting.

Breast—Very wide, very deep, well rounded at the sides, full projecting forward beyond wing fronts when speciment is standing erect; feathers are short, tucked between wings at sides.

Keel—Long, strong, free from crooks; well tucked up in stern, diverging from the back as it extends forwards in a somewhat curved line, the front end well embedded in flesh, meeting a very full swelled chest.

Body and Stern—Body, well rounded at sides; feathers, short; stern well tucked up; feathers, scant, very short and tight-fitting.

Wings—Short, very stout, powerful, closely folded; shoulders nearly level or slightly drooping to harmonize with slope of the back; wing fronts standing out prominently from the body at the shoulders; wing points somewhat rounded, but well converged at extreme ends when folded; closely tucked at ends and held about on a line with lower tail coverts or slightly wider.

Tail—Short, compact, closely folded when the specimen is standing at ease, carried nearly horizontally, slightly drooping preferred.

Legs and Feet—Legs, straight, not more than slightly bent at hock joints when specimen is standing easily erect; thighs of medium length, round, thick, stout, bulging with muscular development, set wide apart; shank, short, well rounded, stout in bone, smoothly scaled, standing evenly and well apart. Feet, large, flat; toes, strong, rather thick, medium in length, straight, well spread, the hind toes set low and extending backward; nails, strong and well shaped. Shanks, feet and toes, free from feathers and down.

Plumage—Short, narrow, hard, wiry, very glossy.

Body in Hand—Firm, compact, very muscular.

Station, Carriage and Style—Station moderately low, carriage and style very erect, upright, commanding, giving an appearance of great vigor; alert, graceful in movements.

Size—The specimen should be of sufficient size to possess Standard weight in normal breeding condition.

Color of Dark Cornish Male

Head—Plumage, greenish-black.

Beak—Yellow.

Eyes—Yellow, or approaching pearl.

Face—Bright red; plumage, black.

Comb, Wattles and Earlobes—Bright red.

Neck—Hackle, glossy greenish-black, shafts, red, plumage, other than hackle, glossy greenish-black, free from any other color, except shafts next to fluff which may be red or black, red preferred.

Back—Each feather possessing a more or less irregular center of dark red, surrounded by a decided predominance of glossy greenish-black; shafts, next to fluff, red, saddle feathers, like back in color, but with a somewhat larger proportion of dark red which may partake of the form of striping.

Breast and Body—Glossy greenish-black, free from any other color, except shafts next to fluff, which may be red or black, red preferred.

Stern—Black.

Wings—Wing fronts, greenish-black; wing bows, each feather possessing a more or less irregular center of dark red, surrounded by a decided predominance of glossy greenish-black; shafts, next to fluff, red; coverts, forming wing bars, glossy greenish-black, with shafts next to fluff, red or black, red preferred; primaries, black, except a narrow edging of bay on outer web, secondaries, upper web, black, lower web, about one-third black next to shaft, the remainder being bay.

Tail—Greenish-black; sickles and coverts, glossy greenish-black.

Legs and Feet—Thighs, greenish-black except shafts next to fluff which may be red; shanks, feet and toes, orange and yellow.

Under Color—Dark slate. In the descriptions of Breast and Body, the red of the "shafts next to fluff" is not intended to extend out onto the shafts next to the web or the surface portion of the feather. Males with red shafts, in the slate under-color frequently possess the best hackle striping and often prove the best breeders or progeny of either or both sexes

Color of Dark Cornish Female

Head—Plumage, greenish-black.

Beak—Yellow.

Eyes—Yellow, or approaching pearl.

Face—Bright red; plumage, black.

Comb, Wattles and Earlobes—Bright red.

Neck—Hackle, glossy greenish-black, with rich golden-bay shaft to each feather, the black greatly predominating; plumage, other than hackle, ground color, rich golden-bay, not faded, each feather having two pencilings of glossy greenish-black, narrow to medium in width, never broad, feather uniformly free from heavy black tips; the outermost bay more nearly oval than angular toward the end and the center bay of good width.

Back, Breast, Body, Wing Bows, Wing Coverts, Tail Coverts—Ground color, rich golden-bay, not faded, each feather having two pencilings of glossy greenish-black, narrow to medium in width, never broad, the pencilings following the contour of web of feather uniformly, free from heavy black tips; the outermost bay more nearly oval than angular toward the end and the center bay of good width.

Stern—Black, or black tinged with bay.

Wings—Primaries, black except a narrow edging of irregularly penciled bay upon outer part of web; secondaries, upper web black, lower web black next to shaft of feather, with a broad margin of irregularly penciled bay.

Legs and Feet Thighs, black more or less shafted with bay, but solid black not a serious defect; shanks, feet and toes, orange and yellow.

Under Color—Dark slate.

(The above Standard compiled by W. S. Templeton)

Cornish Bantams

The following Standard for Cornish Bantams was suggested by Courtland H. Smith, Warrenton, Va., in 1916 and published in the American Cornish Club Annual Year Book. Mr. Smith has had much success in breeding Bantams and has made a half pound reduction in weights from that required by the English Standard.

Dark and White Cornish Bantams

Disqualifications—Same as for large Cornish; also, cocks weighing over three and one-half (3½) pounds; hens over three (3) pounds, cockerels over three (3) pounds, and pullets over two and one-half (2½) pounds.

Standard Weights

Cocks, 2½ lbs
Hens, 2 lbs
Cockerels, 2 lbs.
Pullets, 26 oz.

Shape and Color of Male and Female

The general shape and color of Dark and White Cornish Bantams shall be the same as the Standard for the large birds.

CHAPTER III

DARK CORNISH

The Result of Enthusiasm—During the last four decades the Cornish fowl has been led by the Dark variety. There are more Dark Cornish bred in America and England than any of the other Cornish varieties. The White, Buff and White Laced Red Cornish have each many enthusiastic breeders who have developed them to their present high standard.

Because the early history of the Dark Cornish fowl is obscure and because the breed did not attract attention until about 1886, it may be questioned whether the breed can be considered other than a modified Aseel fowl, as pointed out in the chapter on the origin and history of Cornish.

In the early days there was no definte Cornish type. The birds varied greatly in markings—some being single and some triple laced—in weight, and in style and carriage. Many were low and blocky Aseel types, and others were tall and rangy Malay types, with gradations between the two.

When the Dark Cornish variety was first introduced in America, there were many fanciers who could not dissociate the word "game" from the Exhibition Black-Breasted Red Game. They insisted upon patterning birds after the latter. There were only a few early breeders who advocated the low, blocky Aseel type The type now seen in show rooms corresponds to the low station birds. The English fanciers quite approach our ideal in this respect and breed birds of the low and blocky type.

The American Poultry Association has not grouped the different breeds geographically, otherwise the modern Cochin, the Spangled Hamburg, and the Exhibition Game would be placed in the English class. As the geographic origin has not been considered by the A. P. A., it is the group characteristics that have ruled. In short, the Asiatics are so classed because they have certain traits in common, and not because they all came from Asia. It is the same with the Mediterranean class and the English class. But the Dark Cornish breed in no way follows this rule. It has been placed in the English class, but there is a great contrast between the Cornish breed and the other members of the English class, examples of which are the Orpington and Dorking fowls.

Reclassification—The Dark, and all the other Cornish breeds of distinctly American origin properly belong in the Oriental class. If the breed does not follow the characteristics of the English class, it naturally follows that in its treatment in the show room by a judge of miscellaneous poultry, confusion could arise in placing the awards. As a matter of fact, it has been placed in the English class in order to get it on the main floor with other popular breeds in the English class, instead of being relegated to the A. O. V. class.

It is believed that the increased demand for exhibition birds

MODERNIZED CORNISH

" CLAMOROUS " represents the present type of Cornish. He is a champion of repute, having won first honors while a cockerel and later as a cock at leading shows.

stopped the breeding, to some extent at least, for fighting qualities. Traces of old English Game blood can no longer be found in the modern Cornish. As the demand for table qualities became more pronounced, the size of the fowl increased, the plumage softened, and the legs lengthened by the introduction of blood of some non-game, soft-feathered breed as the Langshan. This anglicization was most noticeable in the early 90's, and it included all the British strains as well as those still claiming to be East Indian.

Reversion to Type—About 1900 or a little earlier, there was a reversion to type of the fowl, and the low, blocky station became noticeably Oriental; so much so, that the original Aseel was excelled.

The markings of the Dark Cornish male are decidedly characteristic. The feathers are a lustrous greenish-black color, mixed with a dark red color in the neck, wings and back. In the neck and hackle, only the shafts are dark red; while in back, the greenish-black predominates over the dark red. The breast is a lustrous greenish-black. The tail is black, with the sickles and coverts greenish-black. The under-color in all sections is dark slate. The shanks and the skin are a rich yellow. The eyes are yellow to pearl in tint.

The female has more color than the male. She has a greenish-black head, yellow beak and bright red face, comb, wattles and earlobes. The feathers have a deep bay shaft. The front of the neck approachs a rich mahogany hue, each feather having two pencilings of lustrous black following the contour of the feather. The bows and coverts are bay approaching mahogany, the feathers being penciled in the same manner as the neck feathers. The primaries are black and have an irregular penciling of bay on the outer part of the web. The same penciling is found on the lower section of the web on the secondaries, the upper webs being black. The main tail feathers are black with the two upper ones irregularly penciled with a bay tint. The under-color of all sections is dark slate.

The Head of the Male Bird—The head of the Dark Cornish male bird is short, very broad between the eyes and has a thick and broad occipital bone. The beak is very strong and short, the lower mandible being thick and straight, while the upper mandible is thick and strongly curved. The face has a fine texture, though it is tough in substance. The earlobes are very small and very close to the head. The wattles are small or even lacking.

The bold, brilliant eyes, set back in the head, are of a pearl or yellow pigment, and the small upright pea comb is tough in substance.

The neck of the male bird is round, hard and muscular; of medium length and slightly curved. As it descends, it broadens out into a short, full breast, carrying no fluff and almost naked at the point of the breast bone and projecting beyond the tips of the wings. In the back, the neck broadens out at the shoulders where it is filled in with strong musculature. From the nape of neck, the back slopes back and downward to the tail, and there is a gradual slope from the angles of the ribs on either side of the spine. The wings are short, strong and carried neatly and compactly out from the shoulders in line with the tail feathers, and often show a bare spot at the first joint.

The stern is narrow in comparison with the shoulders. It is thick and strong at the root of the tail, this being an indication of great strength. The tail feathers are short and slightly drooped; they are narrow and hard in texture. The sickles are very fine, hard and short, tapering like a scimitar three or four inches from the ground. The coverts are short, narrow and wiry.

The short, thick and muscular thighs of the male bird are set wide apart and covered with small feathers. The shanks are also short, but they are smooth and straight with regularly outlined scales. The feet are large and flat and the toes are thick and straight. The duck foot is a serious defect but not a disqualification.

A specimen in fine condition, conforming to type and having symmetrical proportions, is allowed 40 points on the scale of points when judged by comparison, with a possible five points for the plumage, which should be very glossy, hard in texture, close and wiry.

THE CENTURY'S SENSATION

The "20th CENTURY MODEL" has been one of the biggest attractions at the leading shows in America, including club meets held by the American Cornish Club. She stands without a peer in the annals of Cornish.

The Distinctive Type—The type of the bird is distinctive, being very muscular, compact and heavy for its size and appearance. The station is moderately low; the carirage is very erect, upright and commanding, giving an appearance of strength and vigor. Altogether, the Dark Cornish male bird, may be taken as typifying the male Cornish Standard of the other three varieties.

Physical Make-up of the Female—The physical make-up of the female Dark Cornish is much like that of the male. The throat is fuller and dotted with small feathers. The whole general appearance of the female resembles that of the male, giving the impression of sturdiness, but the coloring is higher and has more penciling, while the tail lacks the scimitar-like sickles of the male. The head is large, and the expression often stern and forbidding, with a certain venomous gleam in the light-colored eyes. Some, however, particularly those that have been imported, or are the progeny of an English and American cross, have a stolid smug appearance resembling the pug dog rather than the bulldog.

Special disqualifications of the Dark Cornish fowl are to be found mainly in the coloring. Solid white, blue or black shanks are serious disqualifications.

The Under-color—The full measure of popularity that is due birds of recognized standard is marred somewhat by the idea that a light under-color, principally in the female, affects unfavorably the color of the plumage. According to the present standard, a light under-color is considered a defect. It is believed that the customary prejudice against white in the under-color has prevented many otherwise prize-winning birds from winning at our leading shows. It is claimed by some that the breed would gain even greater popularity if a light under-color were made a Standard requirement.

W. S. Templeton, of California, one of the pioneer breeders of Cornish, states the following about color marking in an article entitled " Color Markings of Dark Cornish Female " which appeared in the American Cornish Club Year Book, 1915:

> The Ideal—" The ideal, as I understand it, is a more or less visionary perfection toward which nature will consent to work in harmony with man to attain the reality in form, feather, color, markings. Nature has certain well established laws and if man's mental ideals are in accord with these laws, nature may be induced to produce living models. Just as soon as man sets up imaginary requirements that are contrary to these laws, his artistic portraits and word pictures cease to represent genuine ideals, for nature cannot and never will follow and where nature refuses to be led the ideal does not exist It may, therefore, be seen that the so-called standard of any breed may represent a perfect ideal, or,the next best, an imperfect ideal, if it isn't a complete failure. As man does not understand all of nature's laws, it is safe to assert many standards do not fulfill the purpose for which they were intended, while some are actually antagonistic to nature's ideals and impossible of attainment.
>
> " Accept the color description for Dark Cornish female in the 1910, 1912 and 1915 Standards of Perfection as your guide and you will never be able to produce a single specimen that will be perfectly marked in all sections according to that standard which requires two pencilings exclusively in all sections, regardless of the feathers.

Lacings vs. Pencilings—"As this may be read by English as well as American breeders, perhaps I should explain that in England the lustrous greenish-black markings of the female are known as lacings, while in America these markings are now called pencilings. As a matter of fact, the outside or marginal markings of black is lacing; for a lacing is always on the edge of a feather, while

A WINNER

A splendid specimen of Dark Cornish. This male bird was a winner every time shown, both in this country and in Europe.

the inside marking of black is a penciling, since a crescentic penciling is always away from the edge of a feather, as in the Partridge and the Silver Penciled varieties, such as the Dark Brahma female.

"Look among your females for one that is perfectly marked, according to the American Standard of Perfection, on her large feathers, including the wing-coverts, tail-coverts, the back feathers approaching the tail, as well as on lower breast and body feathers back of thighs. The outside lacing of each of these feathers should be very even and moderately narrow, exposing considerable ground color (mahogany) on the natural surface of the plumage. The one inner penciling, crescentic in form and paralleling the lacing, should sub-divide the mahogany ground color into two parts, the central or shaft mahogany being about the same width as or slightly wider than the outermost or crescentic mahogany, which is between the lacing and the penciling. This is theoretically perfect, according to our standard, and we have all been striving to breed females with these large feathers perfectly double marked and all of the small feathers just as nearly ideal. But on such females the small feathers do not come perfectly marked. Instead, we find on the wing-bows, upper breast and neck feathers above the breast as well as on the small back and body feathers, the central bay is entirely too narrow. The shaft alone may be red with no mahogany extending out on either side into the web as it should. This is the reason the exclusively double marked female can never have ideally marked feathers throughout.

"But you can take this same female and you may be able to find among her daughters some having the small feathers ideal in markings. And just as soon as you succeed in breeding ideal small feathers, you will find the central mahogany of the large feathers has increased in width to such an extent that there has crept into the center an additional black marking enclosing a part of the shaft toward the base. This is a rather pointed penciling or stripe. Double markings for the small feathers and triple markings of black for the large feathers are, therefore, nature's ideal for Dark Cornish females, the American Standard of Perfection to the contrary.

The Past History—"Americans ought to know now, for we have tried nearly everything but the ideal, beginning with 'one or more narrow lacings' in 1892, 'two or more narrow lacings' in 1893, 'two narrow pencilings' in 1898 ,and 'two pencilings' in 1905, the latter continuing even to-day. I have quoted this bit of history that no one may think I am advocating the old-fashioned markings which were known as 'triple pencilings,' for nothing is farther from my wish When the Standard in America read, 'two or more narrow lacings,' breeders went to the extreme They allowed triple markings in the small feathers, consequently the females deteriorated into very dark specimens, losing in popularity, and no one has ever accused me of favoring that kind.

"The English Standard, adopted in 1896, is, in some respects more nearly perfect than ours It carries out the general idea that the female should be 'double laced,' but adds: 'and often in the best specimens there is an additional mark enclosing the base of the shaft of the feather and running to a point .' The way the English Standard is written this third marking could hardly appear on the small feathers. Breeders having well marked specimens will have no difficulty in verifying my remarks as to the proper number of markings in each section to obtain ideal color proportions throughout, for the size of the feather governs the number of markings to the greatest extent. A little observation and comparison should dismiss all doubt, especially if one prefers to be a naturalist rather than a theorist.

"A pullet being naturally a little darker, my idea is that her lacings and pencilings should be of about the same width as, but certainly not any wider than, her mahogany markings. After she has moulted as a hen these black markings should be somewhat narrower than the corresponding markings of mahogany, that she may display on the naturally exposed surface of her plumage nearly equal proportions of each other. I have observed these are the birds that more often win under the best judges than the exclusively double marked specimens. But as many of us have been trying to breed the 'exclusively double,' I hope what has been written shall not prove in the least disturbing. Do not sacrifice any good exclusively double marked females, remembering it is still our standard, if not ideal, and not forgetting that some of their daughters and more of their granddaughters will be marked more nearly ideal, for, in spite of all efforts to keep them exclusively double, the triple markings have very naturally persisted in cropping out on the large feathers. It will ever be thus, for it is a mathematical necessity of nature and God has doubtless ruled it so.

The Value of Single Lacing—"For the same reason, I would value an extra good single laced hen as a breeder. This is one that has no penciling within the mahogany. Some of my critics claim such hens are worthless because they produce birds having faded or washed-out bay for ground colorings, which, I admit, is sometimes all too true. However, I have observed these same critics are pretty good patrons of Mr. Wm. Brent's (England) stock, and, as I don't know of any one who has bred or sold more prize winners during the past 35 years than Mr. Brent, it might be interesting to hear what he has said on this subject. I quote from his letter under date of January 8, 1914: '...... if you want to maintain TYPE and clear GROUND COLOR, you must not disqualify some single laced feathers in some sections of the hen's body.' Mr. Brent underscored type and ground color.

"The fact that American breeders persist in refusing to use these extra good single laced hens in their breeding pens may be one reason why they have to part with so much good money to secure the type from England. After all, remember that. 'Type makes the breed, color the variety,' and the one thing paramount in Cornish is TYPE. It requires vigor and stamina to maintain that type If you do not have them, you do not have good Cornish, I care not how good the color and markings may be."

Type vs. Color—Mr. Templeton believes that type in Cornish is as important as the color markings and in his articles in the annual year book of the American Cornish Club of 1917, he explains that sacrificing type for color would ruin his interest in Cornish. He writes further about feather markings:

"We may divide the feather into three or four parts. First, there is the stem that is composed of the quill and the shaft which merge and extend to each extremity Then there is the fluff that begins where the quill and shaft merge and to which we look for the under-color. Finally, there is the web upon which we see the surface color ..

"Let us first get a fair idea of the correct forms of markings of the female Dark Cornish In constructing a garment, it isn't customary to begin with the lace, however, I may be better understood if I begin with the lacing of the feather which is always on the edge, never elsewhere. Take, therefore, a breast feather of medium size, plucked form a hen two to four years old. A lustrous greenish-black lacing three thirty-seconds to a scant one-eighth of an inch wide, but of even width throughout, should form the margin or border of the web That is, beginning at the fluff on one side of the feather, this lacing should extend around the edge of the web until it meets the fluff at the other side where it merges into the under-color. Next to and just within this lacing is a band of rich mahog-any a trifle wider than the lacing. This mahogany band takes the same crescentic form as the lacing and ends at the fluff, its width should be the same throughout, except, possibly, where it ends near the fluff, it narrows. Next in order is a crescentic penciling of lustrous greenish-black which should run parallel to the lacing and of about the same width as the latter Within the penciling, there should be a rather elongated oval center of rich mahogany. This mahogany center should be about five thirty-seconds of an inch wide for the medium sized feather of breast and body, but possibly a trifle nar-rower for medium wing feather since the feather itself may be a little narrower. Where the penciling intersects the shaft I think the latter should be black, but within the mahogany center and extending to the quill, I prefer a very dark red. The fluff or under-color should be moderately dark slate.

Color in Moderation—" As I am a believer in moderation rather than excess, I think the web of a feather from a fully matured female should carry about equal amounts of mahogany and green-ish-black, and, as the lacing has a greater circumference than the mahogany band within it, while the penciling has also a greater circumference than the mahogany center, the mahogany markings may cover as much surface. This for the feathers of medium size. Theoretically, it may appear nearly perfect for feathers of all sizes but it does not work out that way according to nature and mathe-matics If you get such proportionate markings on the lower breast feathers and on the wing-coverts, being large feathers, the mahog-any center may be one-fourth inch wide, but by the time you get in the smaller feathers of the upper breast, fore part of the neck and the smaller feathers of wing-bows and shoulders, the little mahog-any centers will have narrowed out of all proportion, or may be absent entirely, the shaft being either red or black. We will all agree these little feathers, so marked, are not ideal, yet we always get them when we try to follow the American Standard by not having more than two black markings on the largest feathers. I like the English Standard much better in this respect. The idea it con-veys is to get the small feathers alluded to perfectly double marked the mahogany center being at least as wide as either side of the black penciling that surrounds it. Then the medium-sized feathers will be marked about as I have described in this and the preceding paragraph, but in the very largest feathers the mahogany center will have widened to such an extent that an additional marking of black, running to a point, has crept within. This third marking of black applies only to the wing-coverts and the very largest feathers of the lower breast, body, back of thighs and tail coverts. It should never be encouraged elsewhere, for no one wants to go back to the old style, so-called triple laced or triple penciled markings for the general plumage long since out of date

Working With Nature—" If the lacing were proportionately as wide on the large feathers as on the smaller ones, the greater width of the lacing on the large feathers would make that section appear darker. I believe that would be true within certain limitations and where the lacing of the smaller feathers is narrow, as it should be. Nature does permit defects. Indeed, she works with you only when you work with her, for if you work against her your efforts are doomed Take, for instance, the wing Nature strives to have the lacing nearly the same width on all feathers, whether large or small Suppose you start with the wing-coverts and they have the American Standard markings, two of mahogany and two of black, without the black stripe in the center. Now, to get one more viewpoint, we will say the lacing on these large feathers is a bit broad, slightly exceeding one-eighth of an inch in width. With nature, carrying this same width of lacing up to the small feathers, the mahogany in the small feathers is crowded to the center so that this mahogany is practically hidden by the over-lapping feather, with the result that the shoulder part of the wing appears almost black to the observer. I have owned hens with such wings and there is nothing commendable about them I know, at first thought, I have apparently contradicted myself in this paragraph by first stating if conditions could be so-and-so the larger feathers would appear too dark, or darker than the small ones in the same section of the fowl, and then I have turned around and described actual conditions where the small feathers present a darker surface than the larger ones The latter is absolutely true, while the former might be relatively true, and then you should bear in mind I was first discussing medium to narrow lacings, while in the latter I turned to broad or heavy lacings. I hope you understand me. I referred to the former in an attempt to explain why nature demands a third black marking, the stripe, in the very largest feathers In the latter, I presented the folly of heavy lacing, if one wishes the specimen to exhibit uniform color throughout, which is one aim of the fancier.

" As every leaf differs from every other leaf on the same tree, so every feather differs from the others and every fowl has its individuality. Therefore, the reader should not make a too literal application of these views. Some latitude is necessary. Experienced breeders will understand, but beginners may feel a bit confused. To the latter, I would say, to sum up the whole matter briefly, try to get the medium-sized feathers in each section as nearly as possible like the ideal medium sized feather I described and let nature attend to the smaller and the larger feathers. Do not expect the breast feathers to duplicate exactly the wing feathers, or the back feathers those of the body. Every section differs from every other, and yet in a well-bred specimen they all harmonize perfectly.

The Black Color in Pullets—" Should you question why I have confined my remarks to feathers from matured hens, I would say pullets seem naturally inclined to carry a little more black. I would rather not have females of any age heavily laced, but if the black markings of the pullets are not any broader than her mahogany markings, she has an even chance to moult into the sort of a hen we want.

"It is sufficient to add, the back feathers are double marked, while the number of markings on neck-cape and shoulder-capes will be governed by the sizes of the feathers. Possessed of such markings as I have described, the hen's other sections, as neck, wing primaries and secondaries, main tail and thighs, will be marked quite satisfactorily.

"'To produce these markings in the hen's pullets, making due allowance for their carrying a trifle more black until they moult in turn into hens, you may mate her to a Standard marked male, provided his mother and his father's mother possessed similar markings to those you wish to reproduce. Indeed, I should be more particular about the markings of the male's female ancestors than of his own markings A nicely striped hackle is very desirable in a breeding male. In addition, it is preferable to have the shaft down in the fluff red, but the red need not run out upon the shaft in the web to mar the standard black surface color of such sections as breast and body. However, a little more red would not cause me to discard a male, even for breeding exhibition males, for some of his sons would be as dark as we care for. Type being so important in males, judges are inclined to be a bit lenient with a slight excess of red and often such a male's superior type will carry him to victory I am not advocating the necessity of excess red in males, for I believe if your Standard marked males are from females approaching my description you could mate these ideally marked birds together and reproduce them There is no necessity for making a special mating to produce exhibition males and another mating for ideal females......

The Breeder Not a Show Bird—"From the foregoing, it may be understood the best breeder is not always a show bird, while an exhibition specimen may not be a good breeder. One should hesitate to discard a good so-called, single laced hen of exceptional type. Sometimes the use of such a hen will tone up your flock surprisingly in both color and markings as well as type. Experience and a knowledge of the breeding back of each specimen are your best assets, so it is well to trap-nest, toe mark and pedigree the best in your flock.

"It is an easy matter to say we would like the ground color of the richest mahogany, even lustrous, and that we want the lacing and pencilings very lustrous greenish-black, but it is a different proposition to tell you how to avoid faded and peppered bays and purple blacks. In California, I have had strongly colored hens moult in the hot sun in July, when vegetation is none too plentiful and not appetizingly crisp at that, with the result the semi-arid conditions produce disappointing plumage. The ground color would be faded, while the lacings would be a dull black and not clear cut and well defined. Some of these hens would moult the following November and December, while some that had broods of chicks in October and November would moult in January and in every instance under these humid conditions with plenty of vegetation the improvement would be astonishing. The colors and markings would then be as satisfactory as you could obtain anywhere. In Northern Illinois, the summer of 1912 was almost ideal for the development of young Cornish, there being copious rains and no serious dry spells. That year, the young stock had the strongest color I ever saw produced in Illinois, there being almost no white or grey whatever. Twenty-three young trios, along with their parents, were brought to California that November, and the following winter being one of light rainfall in the latter State, the chicks raised from these very strong colored fowls the next spring had more white than I ever saw, there being instances of white on the breast, body, thighs and wings, as well as on the tail. But when the early fall rains set in and crisp vegetation sprang up, the young birds took on new life, developing nicely and moulting into sound colored specimens. Only in a few that appeared to be stunted did there remain evidences of grey.

Parent Stock Not to Blame—"These experiences have taught me a few lessons and we should not be too hasty to blame the parent stock or the young fowls for conditions over which they have no control. The purchaser of a $5, $10 or $15 setting of eggs has often blamed the breeder for the poor results obtained, when the purchaser alone was at fault, probably penning the young birds into a small bare enclosure and expecting them to develop into show birds on a diet of table scraps and grain alone, with enough water to wash the food down and grit to grind it. Fowls must have green food not only for good digestion and strong growth as well as to save more expensive foods, but to make more color pigment, I believe.

"Breeders who live where conditions are arid or sem-arid during the growing and moulting seasons should provide plenty of shade and endeavor to imitate humid conditions by irrigating where possible, or at least provide an abundance of crisp greens and a substitute for the animal matter the birds pick up in bugs and worms in humid countries. To you of the humid sections of the country, when the rains do not come as you wish, I can only say, get out with your hose and make your own rain. Keep something growing, or you will observe during your dry summers and autumns you will be likely to have more trouble with faulty plumage than in wet seasons.

The Three Fundamental Colors—"Even in the best seasons and and with the very best bred stock, we are annoyed with purple. My suspicion is we are demanding an under-color too dark. I have observed, and others have also mentioned it, the males that have the most lustrous dark red and the most lustrous greenish-black do not often run as dark in under-color as the Standard describes.

The Aseels of India that carry such a lustrous green are not very dark in under-color, at least as far as my observations have taken me, and I believe the same is true of the Shamo-Japs of Japan. It is said that the three fundamental colors in the plumage of domestic fowls are red, black and white Some add blue, but others contend the blue in fowls is not a true blue, being a combination of black and white. Then we have the yellow color matter in or under the skin, shanks and toes, and yellow is not very far from green in in the rainbow. Could it be that the combining of a rather light under-color with the black surface would give us a recessive poultry blue and this blue combined with yellow produce the green sheen? And might it be possible that by darkening the under-color the blue is made so dark, so nearly black, that the green is displaced by purple? It would seem that way, and yet, the same blue which when combined with yellow makes green, will also when combined with red make purple. According to the latter, it is a battle between yellow and red. When yellow is master and blends with blue, we get the desired green, but when yellow gets a temporary setback, red blends with blue, and we get the purple. This may account for the purple bars, at least. The cocks that glisten with a green sheen, you will probably notice have bay on the flights or wing primaries that is more inclined toward bright yellow than dark red, though the red in other sections of the bird may be as dark as in any other cocks There will be no harm in breeding for a rich yellow in skin, beak and shanks and then, if your cock birds have brilliant green sheen, you need not throw up your hands in despair should you find their under-color is not quite as dark as you have always thought you would have liked. They are the males to transmit the green to the lacings of their daughters. Remember, it is better to work with nature than against her and you probably cannot get all of the qualities you would like bred into a single Cornish

CHAPTER IV

WHITE CORNISH

An American Production—Pure, uncrossed Dark Cornish never produces a so-called " sport " or albino. But when crossed with other fowls, Cornish does occasionally " throw " an albino type (see chapter on breeding). It is claimed, however, that White Cornish are no other than offsprings of White Malays, which were unloaded in this country during the Cornish boom, when they failed to be sold in England. They were bought here under the name of White Cornish or White Indian Games. Dr. H. P. Clarke says they were " off " on type, and that White Cornish of to-day are an American production. He says there are no White Cornish to speak of in England. The best White Cornish are said to be descended from a White Aseel cock which won first and special prize at the St. Louis World's Fair in 1904 for Dr. Clarke. He believes that all White Cornish can trace their pedigree to this bird.

In the American Cornish Club Annual of 1917, C. Y. Gibbs, of Wayzata, Minn., claims to have been one of three persons in this country to start breeding White Cornish in 1897, and that three years later he exhibited some at the show in St. Paul, Minn., as the "first White Cornish ever seen." He states that the judges recommended more size and better color. He sent a number of birds to the World's Fair at St. Louis and won a number of places, including first pullet. At the show were 21 entries of the " Royal Strain," owned by W. S. Templeton. Mr. Gibbs claims to have introduced in his strain some " northern bred Leghorn blood, which resulted " in an improvement in type and size, shorter legs, better color in old birds, quicker maturity and more practical plumage for the North."

The composition of the variety contains considerable White Malay and Aseel blood with the addition of White Georgia Game and White Wyandotte blood. The latter crosses are supposed to have eliminated many Cornish characteristics, making them tall, narrow fowls. The White Wyandotte cross produced the long soft feather, poor carriage and a " dubbed " comb.

Owing to the strenuous efforts of White Cornish breeders these defects have gradually disappeared, so that the typical Cornish frames, with thick, wide-spread legs and heavy skulls have taken their places in the show room.

Possesses Desirable Qualities—This variety embodies in its Standard requirements which were made in 1898, a shape which not only makes a distinct variety of Cornish, but also establishes an ideal type for meat production. It is supplemented by a hardy, vigorous constitution, clothed in a coat which conceals no bodily weaknesses. Color is more uniformly attained than type.

Many breeders have attempted to mate birds for color alone and have slighted sections which contributed to Cornish qualities. Many have neglected the importance of bodily vigor, weight and shape, which are the very foundation of the breed. Birds showing these qualities must be bred in preference to others. Consideration of color also is, of course, essential.

WHITE CORNISH

This pair is representative of the popular variety now engaging the attention of poultrymen in general.

"Ticking" in the plumage must be carefully avoided. but creaminess should not be considered sufficient cause to eleminate any bird if it has good type and shape. As long as the requirements are for yellow shanks and beak, with pure white plumage, brassiness and the creamy tinge in the plumage is bound to occur. This can be somewhat eradicated by breeding for a lighter color of yellow in the shanks and beak. It will be noticed that birds with white shanks and beaks usually have pure white feathers, and as a rule the darker the shanks and beaks the more brassy the plumage. The pigment in yellow corn is said to color the feathers, but this is similar to the school girl's superstition that carrots are good for the complexion.

The Standard requirements for this variety are the same as those for the Dark variety. The color requirements are th same as those for any of the white feathered fowls. Solid white, blue or black legs are disqualifications, also foreign colored feathers.

The use of White Cornish as a utlity fowl is apparent. As a market fowl its yellow skin gains favor with the fastidious buyer of dressed poultry. It is valuable for crossing on other white breeds to enhance carcass size; and it will stamp the Cornish type on two-thirds of its offspring. With the introduction

A TYPICAL SPECIMEN

A White Cornish male. Breeders are now building up this variety to compare favorably with the Dark Cornish in type.

of Leghorn and Wyandotte blood egg production increases, with large tinted eggs.

Selecting Breeders—In the selection of breeders it is well to keep in mind that weight, size of bone, broad skulls, backs and breasts on both material and paternal sides make type a feature. Many buy a good male and expect the offspring from mates that have not been selected to liken the male. See the chapter on breeding.

The average White Cornish has a long back which helps them in the production of eggs. Long thin bills give the whole head the appearance of slenderness and detract from an otherwise broad skull. Loose feathers take the variety entirely out of the Cornish class. Some have concluded that length of leg and brassiness of feathers seem to be essential for weight; in which case they believe it would be well to have brass and reduce the legs at a little sacrifice of weight which could be made up from the female side of the mating.

Type vs. Color—In an article in the 1916 year book of the American Cornish Club, entitled, "Breeding White Cornish," by

W. Miller Higgs, Victoria, B. C., the following thoughts were given: Purity of color and type are the two great difficulties in breeding. A pen purchased by the writer were pure in color, but not typical of the breed. They were fine layers because of an ʳdmixture of Leghorn blood. Another trio was imported from England. They resembled White Aseel fowls. The male bird was brassy in color, low to the ground and possessed of compactness of bone. One hen was decidedly Aseel and the other was more typically Cornish. With these birds properly mated to birds of the first pen, the writer improved the birds in Cornish type.

From a friend, he obtained two black "sports," of a White Cornish mating with beautiful lustrous green sheen, black legs, but with an inclination to yellow under the feet, a thick tail, good backs, but not wide between the shoulders, good heads and gullets. Mating with the offspring of the foreign and domestic birds produced birds some of which were white, some black and others which were either silver-laced or golden-laced of fine Cornish type No black cockerel was ever hatched from these matings, (a fact known to exist in genetics). The writer claims to have produced some very typical White Cornish from these matings. It is thought that the black hereditary unit, possibly Black Java blood, was just enough to overcome the brassiness which is usually so difficult to combat in the males and the tendency to creaminess in the under-color of the females.

The Mendelian factors for coloring account for the above incident in that the black or perhaps a mahogany color acts as a check in feathers of a solid color. This factor is doubtless inherent in the chromosomes of the fertilized egg.

CHAPTER V

BUFF CORNISH

The Vogue in Buff Color—Very little has been written on this newer American variety of Cornish which has gradually worked its way forward and is now being shown at our best poultry exhibitions.

The popular buff color no doubt excited the Cornish breeders to the end that they proceeded to make a Buff variety. That success has been attained goes without saying, for we now have a very typical Cornish with beautiful buff color.

There were in different parts of the country breeders who were working upon the same idea, which was crossing Buff Plymouth Rocks and Buff Wyandottes upon both White and Dark Cornish. In some instances Buff Leghorn, Buff Cochin and Buff Orpington blood was infused to establish color more firmly. The history of the origin dates back to the spring of 1906.

It developed that the Leghorn infusion naturally had a tendency to a higher egg production, but at the same time this cross did not attain the desired weight. Still, the offspring were well fleshed and showed much activity.

The Successful Crosses—The Buff Plymouth Rock and Wyandotte crosses were more of a success, and it is natural to suppose that our present day strains are of a larger percentage of this cross than of the Leghorn.

Buff Cornish compare very favorably with the other varieties of Cornish in body and type, having deep breasts, broad shoulders, legs thick and wide apart, somewhat longer bodies, and the distinctive low pea comb and broad skull of the breed. It seems probable that the best results with this newer addition to the family would be obtained by out-crossing to gain the rich buff color and by line breeding to establish Cornish type.

There is much still for the fancier who takes up this variety. As with other Buff breeds the ideal buff color comes only through untiring patience in breeding operations, and careful study. But buff color is so immensely popular with American fanciers that any variety of a breed possessing it is bound to remain among the leading races of domestic poultry, provided, of course, it meets the other necessary requirments which make up the much-sought after but rarely found general purpose fowl.

The Standard Requirements—While no official standard has ever been adopted for this variety, the general consensus of opinion coming from the breeders of Buff Cornish, is that they should conform to the standard made for the other varieties of Cornish as to type, and to the color standard of other Buff breeds, especially the Buff Orpington.

Winning males at some of our largest exhibitions have weighed 10 pounds and over, and females 7 pounds and up. With strict attention to the rudiments which govern the breeding of the Dark and other varieties of the Cornish family, the time is not far off when we shall see Buff Cornish holding a popular place.

There are many prominent breeders of this variety. All have made use of the Buff Rock, Buff Wyandotte, Buff Leghorn and Rhode Island Red crosses in some form or other with equally good success.

CHAPTER VI

WHITE LACED RED CORNISH

Developing a Modern Fowl—This breed of Cornish was originated and named by W. H. Card, Manchester, Conn., about 1898. His purpose was to develop a fowl with the best qualities of all the breeds, such as large amount of good meat, egg-production, yellow skin and light under-color that would leave no dark pin feathers.

THE STANDARD TYPE

This strain originated by W. H. Card possesses lacing in the hackle. This type is recognized by the American Poultry Association.

He used as the foundation of this new breed a peculiar looking pair of birds of Cornish type, but buff in color, with a few white spots in the hackle, white tails and flights ,and a blueish white under-color. This pair was the product of a Shamo-Japanese fighting game fowl. The results of this mating were peculiar markings and a blueish under-color. This foundation stock was crossed on the offspring of a Dark Cornish and Light Brahma. The pullets produced were mated with a White Indian cockerel and a White Wyandotte cockerel; one for the purpose of producing good egg laying qualities, and the other for meat.

In 1900, Mr. Card mated the best cockerel sired by the White

Indian male with the best pullets of the other cross; but these were lacking in size, and all but three cockerels and one pullet were killed. The 1899 White Indian male was bred in 1901 to the one lone pullet and the best hen of the Wyandotte mating.

In 1902, he began to inbreed. In 1899 male was mated back to his own pullets of the 1900 hatch. In 1903 he mated the 1899

JUBILEE CORNISH

Practically unknown in America. Likely a cross between White Cornish and Black-Breasted Red Game.

male to his pullets of the 1902 hatch. In 1904 the 1899 cock was bred to his largest and best daughters of the 1903 hatch, regardless of lacings or color.

That same year, 1904, a dark colored cockerel hatched in 1903 was mated to a few of the best hens of the 1901 and 1902 hatch. In May, 1904, at the suggestion of W. S. Templeton, then of Dakota, Ill., the 1899 male was placed with two Dark Cornish females. The best male of this cross was used on the 1904 pullets which had been sired by the 1899 male from his own daughters of the 1903 hatch. These females carried fifteen-sixteenths (15-16) of the blood of the 1899 sire, making him a great-great-grandfather of his own daughter.

Fixing Color and Markings—This mating fixed his color and marking characteristics and established this color scheme as a variety of Cornish quite distinctive. It left one-sixteenth (1-16) of the blood's element to atavistic tendencies.

After 20 years of consistent breeding this variety has become very popular. It breeds true to type, white lacings and white under-color, a heritage from the two white breeds and the Shamo-Japanese in the original matings. Pigment in the feathers of this variety results from the color factor in the Mendelian law, that is, the mixture of the pure white with the dark (not black) unit characters, producing, " .... the reddish quill; from the skin to the lacing it is snow white; and the red pigment which shows is localized in the center of this characteristic white lacing, so that there is no connection between the red surface and the skin except the reddish quill."

THE EARLY TYPE

White Laced Red Cornish, as they appeared at the time they were admitted to the American Standard of Perfection in 1909.

The Chicks—The chicks hatch a primrose color, but their first feathers are white and remain that way from 6 to 16 weeks. Moulting adult birds also have the same change in color, starting with a white moult and gradually increasing to red as it advances. The pigment is a deep rich red, and by being narrowly and accurately laced with white in every section from head to tail, in both the made and female, it makes a beautiful contrast with the snow-white under-color. The tail feathers are white with a red shaft.

There are imperfections in the color markings which often discourage the beginner. Sometimes the neck and shoulders only are laced. Sometimes the birds are well laced except for the breast. Occasionally double lacing appears and in some cases the spangled effect crops out. Atavistic tendencies are shown by an occasional throwing back of the offspring to a Dark Cornish or a White Cornish " sport " or albino. These unexpected changes which come with growth and moult often keep the breeder guessing as to what he may expect when he is not sure of the blood lines possessed by the ancestors.

Obtaining the Lacing—The infusion of Dark Cornish blood brings out exceptional Cornish type in the offspring. It often produces females splendidly laced in every section but the neck

THE TEMPLETON CALIFORNIA STRAIN

This strain of White Laced Red Cornish possesses no lacing in the hackle. They are supposed to be an off-spring of the cross between a Dark and White Cornish.

which is white to the head. The males from similar matings show white hackles until maturity when they suddenly change to bright red with white lacings. Such birds breed white necked females.

In order to overcome the tendency to the lack of lacing in the neck, dark red males with scanty lacings on hackle, back and saddle are used in mating to white necked females. It invariably regulates the color and preserves the type.

Exhibitions of White Laced Red Cornish within the last few years have produced birds of unquestionable Cornish type in every respect. They no longer show the Leghorn back that a few years since was so noticeable. The breeders have used males that possess short saddle feathers on females with the same characteristic, the males being from the shortest saddle feathered females, to overcome this fault.

Varieties in Lacing—The American Standard of Perfection gives the color markings of the neck of this variety of Cornish as possessing a laced hackle. There has been another strain which is without the lacing in the neck. Both have their enthusiastic followers. The latter is supposed to be the offspring of a cross between a Dark and White Cornish. There is also another variety of somewhat similar markings which is practically unknown in America, but is designated in England as the Pile or Jubilee Cornish. This is likely a cross between the White Cornish and Black-Breastd Red Game intensified by a few seasons of inbreeding. They are an extremely beautiful variety, white where the other (Dark Cornish) variety is black or lustrous greenish-black. The males are sometimes black, except for a slight red edging to the wing bays. Th under-color is very light. " The Feathered World " (London), December 31, 1920, ran a cut of a Jubilee Indian Game cock and hen, drawn by R. E. Steed, author of the article in the same issue, entitled " Jottings from a Poultry Keeper's Sketch Book."

For the correct color markings of the White Laced Red Cornish and points of disqualification, the reader is urged to obtain the latest edition of the American Standard of Perfection. The shape is the same as that given for Dark Cornish male and female.

CHAPTER VII

MATING AND BREEDING CORNISH

The Application of Biological Laws—Breeding has become one of the most interesting, and at the same time, one of the most profitable phases of the livestock industry. Biologists have given us many helpful pointers, and the results obtained and published by successful breeders have made it possible for anyone of average intelligence to breed Cornish successfully.

The Mendelian theory of heredity has been found to hold true by recent experiments. It can be best explained by showing the result of original work along this line.

It is convenient for brevity to use some of the technical terms used by biologists. That the reader may understand the significance of the terms used, the following definitions are given:

A reproductive cell capable of uniting with another reproductive cell to form a new individual is called a **gamete**.

A **zygote** is the result of the union of two gametes in fertilization, an egg with a sperm. It is actually a new individual produced by a sexual process.

A **homo-zygote** is formed from the union of gametes which transmit the same Mendelian character, as for example, a Dark Cornish joined with a Dark Cornish, or a White Cornish joined with a White Cornish.

The **hetero-zygote** results from the union of gametes which transmit different Mendelian characters as Dark Cornish united with White Cornish.

Unit-characters are characters which follow Mendel's law of heredity, i. e., are inherited as independent units.

These characters differ in succssive generations, so the means of designating the different generations are reckoned from the beginning of the cross or hybridization, in which parents of unlike character are mated with each other. This first cross is called the **parental** generation or P generation. Subsequnt generations are called **filial generations** (abbreviated F), and their numerical order indicated by a subscript, as first filial (F1), and second filial (F2), etc.

Striking Uniformity in Characters—Pure races when crossed show a striking uniformity in the characters of the first filial generation (F1). Any marked lack of uniformity in F1 indicates an impurity in one or more of the parent blood lines (heterozygous for one or more Mendelian character units). It is then in the F2 generation that characters in which the parent blood lines differ from each other, are recombined by careful selection on the part of the breeder.

It is the number of birds in F2 breeding true to type and color, and the number that do not, that enables the breeder to know how many Mendelizing units distinguish the parental blood lines and what their nature is, whether **dominant** or **recessive**.

These latter terms may be best explained by illustration. If we mate a Dark Cornish (colored) with a White Cornish (uncolored) the offspring will be mostly colored. The colored variety would be, according to Mendel's terminology, dominant in the cross; while the so-called albino (white) recedes from view. Coloring is, therefore, called the dominant character, albinism the recessive.

A FOUNDATION SIRE

" CLAMPIT " headed the famous COOLKENNY strain of Dark Cornish because of his demonstrated prepotency and ancestral make-up.

Practical Demonstration—Practical demonstration of these factors has been made by taking two individuals produced by such a cross as formerly mentioned, and mating them with each other. The recessive (albino or white) character appears on the average of one in four of the offspring. The reappearance of the recessive character after skipping a generation in the proportion of one to four in the second generation of offspring, is a regular feature of Mendelian inheritance.

Accordingly, a female hybrid will transmit the character of color (C) in one-half of its eggs, and the contrasted character of albinism (c) in the other half of the eggs. On the other hand, the male hybrid will also transmit color (C) in half of its sperm, and albinism in the other half (c). If the type of egg which transmits color (C) is fertilized as readily by one type of sperm as by the other, combinations will result which are either two C's or two c's in character. Putting together the results, we get one combination of color with color, two combinations of color with albinism, one combination of albinism with albinism; or three combinations which contain color, and one combination which lacks color, and is therefore all white. This agrees with the average result of any cross of pure Dark Cornish with pure White Cornish. Thy involve no necessary change in type, and merely contain within the race two sharply contrasting colors.

Actual Experimenting—The results are more complicated when parents are crossed which differ simultanously in two or more independent unit-characters. Crossing then becomes an active agency for producing new changes. In order to test out this latter feature of raising pure breeds, a Dark Cornish cock bird three years old was mated with a pure White Cornish hen two years old. The result of this mating was a combination of two colors in each one of the progeny. That is, the plumage was bright red, each feather being tipped with white. The eyes were yellow approaching pearl. The hackle in most was solid white, while some were laced in the hackle. The Cornish type was stamped firmly on each individual. The second generation of this cross produced birds of four types. Some were like one grandparent, some were like the other grandparent, and some were of the white-laced variety; and one seemed to be a " sport " in color and markings, in no way resembling the other progeny. The Mendelian theory of independent unit-characters accounts for this type.

Any breeder who by means of crosses has produced any type or coloring which to him seems to be up to the Standard, or who has produced a new variety, wishes of course to " fix " it in order to obtain a strain that will breed true. He must, therefore, mate individuals that correspond in every desired characteristic in so far as is possible.

A Good Method to Follow—A good method for the breeder of Cornish to follow is to test by suitable matings the unit-characters of each individual that shows the desired combination in type, color and texture of plumage. In this manner a pure blood line may be built up from individuals proved to be pure. Such a method is sure but slow in cases where the desired combination includes two or more dominant characters, for it involves the application of a breeding test to many dominant individuals, most of whose offspring must be rejected. To obtain quicker results it is advisable in practice to breed from all birds which show the desired combination or which more nearly approach the Standard of Perfection, and eliminate from their offspring such birds as do not show that combination. The breed will thus be only gradually purified.

Unless a breeder has been accustomed to dealing with more than two dominant unit-characters, it is best to attempt to " fix " only one dominant character, or at the most two. When a breeder has, let us say, coloring and size to build up, he has about all he can handle. As a rule only one character unit is worked for perfection. With good foundation stock from which to expand, the dominant characters have already been " fixed "; in which case it is only a matter of perpetuating the line and rejecting all those that do not come up to the Standard.

As a rule it is hazardous to attempt to obtain a sudden change in any one department. This process must be gradual. And it requires time and patience. With good blood lines Cornish will breed true.

Difficult to " Fix " the Type—Sometimes a breeder believes he has exhaustd the possibility of greater perfection in his strain and desires to infuse new blood. If he buys a cock bird of whose genealogy he knows little, he may spoil all his previous efforts to build up his strain, by increasing the number of dominant characters. This makes it difficult to " fix " the type.

In calculating the result to be expected from a particular cross it is necessary to consider, not the number of similar characters which the parents possess, but the number in which they **differ.** There are, perhaps, a hundred factors common to both parents to one in which they are observed to differ, but a factor or characteristic only reveals itself by its disappearance or alteration in the individual offspring.

Breeders of any experience realize that birds which look alike often do not breed alike. And it is just this phase of breeding Cornish which makes it difficult. It is essential, therefore, that birds which look or seem alike be distinguished from those which breed alike or breed true.

Line Breeding or Inbreeding—The Mendelian theory of heredity has proved of the utmost value in all branches of the live-stock industry. When applied to so-called inbreeding or line-breeding, the results are remarkable, in every way.

This method of breeding has been practiced for many years with horses, cattle, sheep and swine as well as with poultry. The results are highly successful when the proper methods are pursued, but utterly disastrous otherwise.

Inbreeding is the mating of two closely related individuals. Where haphazard methods are followed and individuals are mated regardless of their vigor and stamina, poor results must inevitably follow. For related individuals are apt to have the same weaknesses and these become more pronounced in their offspring. So that, in a short time of haphazard inbreeding, the stock may be ruined On the other hand, where intelligent selection is made and only the best individuals are allowed to propagate, their good qualities are enhanced in theoffispring. By this method inbreeding proves beneficial and the inbred fowls are rugged and strong.

Shorthorn Cattle an Example—By way of illustration we may cite the work of Amos Cruickshank in the production of

Shorthorn cattle. Mr. Cruickshank was a wealthy Scotch bachelor. His great ambition was to produce Shorthorn cattle that would prove profitable in the untoward conditions in the northeastern part of his country. For twenty-five years he searched the best herds in British yards for animals that approached his ideal. At the end of these years he was disappointed with the result. In his herd of 300 cattle there was a lack of uniformity; there was no " fixed " type. About this time he purchased an old bull and turned him into the pasture with some old cows that he valued. The result of this cross was a bull of the type for which he had been searching. He placed him in the herd and when the calves began to come he knew that he had indeed at last found his ideal. With this start, he began using the blood of this bull whom he called the " Champion of England." He bred him to his daughters and granddaughters and took the sons and crossed them upon their half-sisters. In this way he fixed a type of English shorthorn cattle which is to-day the most popular and economical of that breed.

The Keynote to Success—Inbreeding is the means of establishing line-breeding. Line-breeding is the continuation of a long line of ancestry without the introduction of new or unrelated blood. The keynote to success in line-breeding is the judicious selection of birds to be mated. Thus family traits of form and color are fixed, and undesirable unit characters are driven out. Line-breeding may be called " purity-breeding," as it drives out the undesirable qualities and blends the desirable ones. This is accomplished by pouring the parent blood into the blood of its own progeny and continuing this until the line is established or until there are enough individuals to breed back in safety, being far enough removed in relationship to insure vigor without the introduction of foreign blood. There are many instances where line breeding has been practiced from ten to thirty years and the size, vigor and stamina have been maintained without the aid of outside blood.

How to Begin—In beginning line-breeding, the quickest results are obtained by selecting birds that are the very best of their kind and as nearly alike in type as possible without being related, and mating them.

The second step is to select the best F1 female and mate her back to her sire, at the same time mating the best F1 cockerel back to his dame. This starts two inbreeding lines on the road to purity-breeding or line-breeding. The resulting F2 offspring contain three-fourths of the blood of the sire in one line, and three-fourths that of the dam in the other.

The third step is to mate the best F2 pullet to her sire who is also her grandshire, and the best F2 cockerel to his dam who is also his grandam.

The F3 generation contains seven-eights ($7/8$) of the sire's blood and one-eighth ($1/8$) of the original dam's blood on one side; and seven-eights (⅞) of the dam's blood and one-eighth (⅛) of the original sire's blood on the other.

This completes the first cycle of inbreeding, which, for the preservation of vigor, should not go beyond the three-year limit with the original sire and dam.

Now we are ready to start the second cycle of inbreeding. Mate the best F3 cockerel of the dam-line to the best F3 pullet of the sire line. This forms the foundation of the second cycle which should be followed in the same manner as the first.

By the time the second cycle is completed, wak and undesirable qualities will have been eradicated and the ideal qualities "fixed."

Now an F1 cock may be mated to an F6 pullet. This will conserve vigor almost as much as intelligent out-breeding, and at the same time will obviate any danger from the infusion of foreign blood.

Mating and Breeding—An article appeared in the American Cornish Club Annual Year Book of 1912, entitled "Mating and Breeding Dark Cornish," by W. S. Templeton, Campbell, Cal., the substance of which is as follows:

The oft-repeated phrase "type makes the breed, color the variety," is nowhere so significant as in mating, breeding and judging Cornish. To get this type, first of all we must have great vigor handed down from a strong line of sturdy ancestors No weaklings can possibly contribute to the improvement of our athletic birds with their big full fronts, heavy shoulders, broad backs and wonderful thighs—the bulldog type of poultrydom—all that is the very strongest in every section, separately and collectively.

While we hear of breeders of the solid colored varieties of Rocks, Wyandottes and Orpingtons, making two matings to secure perhaps the concave sweep of back and tail of the male, and a straight line or convex curve for the female, not so with Cornish, for the nearer alike the two sexes are in type the better we like them. Our Standard requires the top line of back to be slightly convex from neck to tail for both sexes, so we have no use for cushion females or birds whose tail feathering begins half way up their backs. To avoid such never breed from a male having long or abundant saddle feathers. Here is the key: Birds having short, tight back feathering are never very loosed feathered in other sections.

With weaklings and loose feathered birds eliminated, we may quickly pass to the more serious defects, including disqualifications. Look carefully for crooked spines, uneven hips, high tails, crooked or wry tails. It is well to watch closely for small feathers on shanks and toes, and between toes, and to cast aside all birds having long shanks and small bone. Discard bowlegs, birds " in " at hock joints and bent or crow-hocked. Birds with faulty legs seem to age rapidly and the legs and feet are very important. Long necks, long beaks, crooked beaks or cross ᴬⁱⁱ .s and decidedly poor combs should all be shunned. Long lean ads with eyes close together and narrow skulls all point to a weak constitution, and birds with flat sides and slipped wings are no more desirable.

Mating for Type—Mating for type is really a matter of eliminating specimens that are farthest from Standard ideals, and then selecting for the male mates that are strong in sections where he is weakest. In this way, we hope to secure young birds which possess the strong points of both parents and are, consequently, an improvement on them. There is also a possibility of some of the young birds proving a sore disappointment in that they may mature with the weak points of both parents very conspicuous, and especially so if the care of the young stock is neglected; not all of the results obtained depend upon the mating, although it is of first importance. Where one can afford, a still better mating and one from which more uniform results may be expected, is to have a male that approaches perfection in all sections, free from the slightest suggestion of a glaring defect, mated to females equally near to perfection in all sections and as uniform as possible. If this method is continued faithfully, with the male line unbroken, it should in ten years produce a family which may rightfully lay claim to being an established strain. New blood is obtained by securing an unrelated or very distantly related hen as nearly like the family females as possible. To this hen we mate our most suitable male and reserve two or three of her pullets which most nearly resemble our family females. When these pullets become two years old, we may mate them to our strongest and best male or males. From this mating we should secure cockerels to head our family pens. Hens generally lay larger eggs, the chicks hatching larger, getting a better, stronger start.

As long as the Cornish breed maintains its supremacy as the best table fowl, it will have an ever-increasing following of ardent breeders. Therefore, the larger the breast, not slighting other sections, the better. We want a breast bone that is quite deep in front and then so much flesh that the point of the breast bone will have a set-in appearance rather than protruding from the flesh. This requires great breadth of breast and a very wide, very full, prominent chest, well rounded. The ideal breast and chest depends, to a great extent, upon a perfect back.

With all this, we want in our breeders style and ease of action which require strength. A small, low tail and a neat pea comb will add to the attractiveness of the bird and are desirable qualities to transmit. In a breeder, the shape of the comb is of more importance than the size—a nice, fair-sized comb being much better than an ugly little one. The cheeks and eyes should be wide apart, the crown projecting somewhat over the eyes, and the eyes rather large and fearless. The beak should be strong and well curved.

Seven Grades in Marking—Color and color markings in fancy matings are interesting studies and experiments. As E. Templeton understands it, the female markings belong to a progressive cycle of seven more or less distinct steps or graduations in markings. Starting with perhaps a solid buff fowl, or a cinnamon buff inclined to dark in wings and tail, the first step brings us to a red fowl with black spangles on the tips of the feathers, but not so pronounced as the spangled markings of the Golden Spangled Hamburg. Both sexes are very similar in markings. The second step gives us a red fowl, each feather laced with black as in Golden Polish, Golden Wyandotte and Single Laced Dark Cornish, the breasts of some of the males being almost as well laced as those of the females. The selection of males darker in neck hackle, breast and body causes the third step, bringing us to our Standard double penciled female, which in reality has one lacing and one penciling within the lacing. Breeding for solid black breasts and bodies in males gives us the fourth step, the females now coming mostly triple penciled, or having two pencilings within the lacing of black. Here the black has gained supremacy over the red, but in the next step we see the red fighting hard to regain its former predominance. We first detect a spreading out or slight intermingling of the two colors in the female and the increasing red in the hackle of the male brings with it a frosting or edging of red around what was formerly the black lacing of the female. This fifth step constitutes partridge markings, as in Partridge Wyandottes. A few partridge marked Dark Cornish females have been bred. The sixth step is an intermingling or mixing of the two colors, red and brown, known as stippling, as in Brown Leghorn females. The red or brown is now dotted with minute spots or particles of black. The seventh and final step is a reversion to the original red or buff fowl, proof of which is noted in the salmon color of some Brown Leghorn females.

The decline in popularity from 1893 to 1898 is sufficient proof that we do not want heavily laced or triple penciled females. A fowl we have to catch and dig down into its plumage to discover its beauty does not make new friends so rapidly as one which looks pretty at a distance of 25 to 100 feet. If a triple penciled female outclasses her competitors in type, let her win because type is more important than color. But where there is no apparent difference in size and type, the double penciled, and even the single laced females should win over the triple penciling and the single laced and double penciled females are more valuable in the breeding pens, unless one wishes to produce a few exhibition cockerels. Double mating is unnecessary. If you mate for exhibition pullets you will find that you will have plenty of exhibition cockerels.

The Standard for Females—A standard based on experience would read something like this for females: Ground color mahogany red, each feather edged with glossy greenish-black following the contour of web of feather. Each feather may have a crescentic penciling of glossy greenish-black running parallel with the lacing and sub-dividing the bay into two nearly equal parts, the central bay being wider. Shafts next to fluff red. For the breast and body of males, it would read something like this: Ground color dark red, heavily and evenly laced with glossy greenish-black, the red covering but a small portion of the feather. Shafts next to fluff, red.

Even as the American Standard of Perfection is to-day, these descriptions are best to follow when mating up breeding pens, but if you do not care to be quite so radical, then by all means select males that have throughout their entire body, neck and wing plumage, shafts that are red next to the fluff or under-color. This does not in any way mar the solid black surface color of the breasts of males, and these red shafts are of considerable value in warding off triple pencilings in females, temporarily at least. Such males generally have better striped hackles and the striped hackle is more important for pullet breeding than for cockerel breeding. Do not let the red in hackle gain a foothold on the tip and the edges of the feathers or the body plumage of the females will come tipped or edged with bay, which would hasten the variety toward partridge markings.

This standard for females requires a narrow lacing and there may or may not be a crescentic penciling within the lacing. That is, there may be a lacing and a large open red center, or a crescentic penciling may sub-divide this center into two nearly equal parts. In other words, single lacing should be allowed as well as our present Standard double penciling.

A pale, faded or washed out shade of bay is undesirable for stock females. Choose mahogany red, dark red or dark brown ground color and for an ideal breeding male, at least five of the ten wing primaries should be edged with a not too light shade of bay. Selecting females with greenish necks is a pretty good way to help retain the greenish lustre on the dark lacings and pencilings, throughout the entire plumage. For under-color, dark slate is about right, although slate tinged with reddish-brown has been seen in a few good specimens. Color of the eye is not so important, but pale yellow or pale blue approaching pearl are to be preferred.

Never sacrifice superior type and vigor for color and markings. The latter do not assist in filling the egg basket, and, aside from yellow skin, are of little value on the table, and that is where intrinsic values count for most.

CHAPTER VIII

REARING CORNISH

Raising Chicks Important—Perhaps the most important phase of poultry raising is the rearing of the small chicks. But there is a step which should not be overlooked by the breeder of Cornish and that is the selection of the eggs from which the chicks are hatched. It must be remembered that not all eggs will produce chicks; and some eggs may produce weak chicks which soon perish.

It is necessary that the eggs that are to be used in hatching either by natural or artificial means should be from stock of known reproducing qualities. With eggs from stock with these qualities one may be assured of success provided the necessary details of incubation are attended to with regularity, thus minimizing the possibility of poor hatches. Year-old cocks or developed cockerels and one to two-year-old hens are best as breeding stock. Pullets' eggs are usually small and sometimes lack fertility. Old birds have been used many times with success. The old Cornish cock bird " Plymouth " was 11 years old at the time of the Boston show in 1916. Many breeders offered to buy him and take a chance on " hand " fertilization.

Uniformity of size and contour of Cornish eggs to be used for hatching is necessary because any deviation indicates weakness in one form or other. Eggs with ridges on them or with peculiar shapes should not be used; life may begin but seldom matures.

Fresh eggs should be used; eggs which are under 10 days old are considered the best for hatching. They should be stored in a cool dry place at a minimum temperature of 45 degrees F. and turned daily until incubation is begun. Freezing is detrimental to hatching eggs.

The Incubator Chicks—If the chicks are hatched in an incubator it is advisable to allow them to remain in the incubator until two days old. They are then taken out, placed in one of the modern brooders and given their first feeding. There are various ideas concerning the first week's feeding; some breeders give only sour milk, pinhead oats, broken rice, grit and charcoal, while others depend on standard brands of chick feed, which are considered very highly by poultrymen in general. They are scientifically prepared by experts and are evenly balanced rations. Water is given from the start, either plain or with sour milk. Water should be placed so that the chicks may obtain it with the least difficulty. For this purpose the small baby chick water fountains are valuable.

The Critical Stage—After the critical stage of the first two weeks is past the feed may be increased. More sour milk is given mixed with stale bread, wheat, middlings and corn meal. The moisture should be partly absorbed so that the feed becomes crumbly. It is fed in the morning and at noon. The mixed baby chick feed may be fed at night. Some form of green food is essential at all times, such as chopped beets or sprouted oats.

Cornish chicks are hardy and grow rapidly. At the age of five or six weeks they have as much flesh and bone as other breeds do at eight and ten weeks. At this time Cornish chicks should be given dry mash into which, about twice a week, meat ground finely may be incorporated.

One of the essential requirements in rearing chicks is to afford as much range as possible. The broods should be out in the sunshine and on Mother Earth, if the weather permits. Never allow chicks to roam by themselves in wet grass or on damp ground. The brooder should be kept clean. Draughts should be eliminated. As the chicks increase in size larger quarters should be provided, because the body temperature of the chick ranges from 104 to 106½ degrees F. and small quarters decrease proper breathing space and hinder growth.

The Secret of Quick Maturity—The secret in bringing Cornish to early and quick maturity lies in the power to keep them growing from the time they are hatched until they have feathered out. And one of the hindrances which is often overlooked in this respect is the presence of vermin, especially when the chicks are reared by a hen. Lice should be fought assiduously. They stop growth as nothing else will. This recalls the history of a prize winning pullet which was in every respect ideal in type and color, but lacked size. The cause of this was that her owner had overlooked the presence of head-lice after he had attempted to rid a brood of lice by only disinfecting the bodies of the chicks. When the real cause was determined, many of the chicks had died. The inference is plain. The chicks should be examined frequently to prevent only a few days' setback in their growth.

As the brood matures, the cockerels and pullets are separated. Suitable housing should be arranged so they will be by themselves. If the cockerels are to be sold as broilers they are placed in fattening pens. It is well to train birds that are allowed free range by feeding them at all times, but especially in the evening, in the house in which they are to roost when they are older.

Shipping Eggs and Chicks—In conclusion a little may be mentioned concerning the shipping of eggs. Breeders in the business of supplying hatching eggs to the public use the regulation containers that are extensively advertised in the poultry magazines. But there are many small breeders who supply a limited number of customers who do not use the regulation container. In this case it is the rule to pack the eggs in carriers which can be purchased at a reasonable sum. A paper strip is pasted over the end to show that it has not been opened in transit. The carrier is then packed in a market basket which has two handles on it and is half full of hay, straw or excelsior. The carrier is tied firmly to the basket, both crosswise and lengthwise;

FOSTER MOTHERS

Caponized Cornish caring for a clutch of chicks.

the basket is then filled with the packing so that the carrier is completely surrounded. Both handles are crossed and tied securely in position, the top of the basket is then covered with burlap and held in position by a stout cord. The name and address of the consignee should be written plainly on a shipper's tag and the consigner's also written on the upper left hand corner, but in smaller letters. In large, conspicuous letters the shipment should be marked " EGGS," or " EGGS FOR HATCHING," or " HATCHING EGGS." The handles on the market basket act as a means of protection against the piling of other boxes or packages during transit.

Large shipments of eggs may be conveniently and safely handled by the use of bushel baskets. Straw or excelsior is used for protection. Eggs packed in this manner with the burlap or muslin over the top should reach the consignee in condition suitable for immediate hatching.

Baby chicks should be shipped in the advertised shipping boxes. Sending chicks in pasteboard boxes or in improvised wooden ones should not be attempted. If they are to travel any great distance, directions should be written on the outside of the crate as to what to do in case of long delay in shipment. If feeding or watering is necessary in transit, the express agent is required to attend to it when so directed.

In sending any chicks or eggs the consigner should always be familiar with the current rules and regulations of the parcel post and express companies.

" COOLKENNY "

CHAPTER IX

HOUSING CORNISH

Types of Poultry Houses—A good poultry house is not necessarily a high priced one. A study of the different types of poultry houses used throughout the country reveals a great lack of uniformity in their construction. It is said that perhaps 90 per cent. of the poultry houses constructed defeat the purpose for which they are built. Often one may witness a flock of birds in disagreeable weather huddled together under the wagon shed or some other building, ignoring the house built purposely for them. Something is wrong evidently with the construction or layout of the building. Birds living under such adverse circumstances do not produce profits, either in meat, eggs, breeding stock or exhibition value.

Locating the House—Location is one of the first considerations in the construction of the poultry house. If the breeder lives in the North where the snow in very deep in winter, the "hen house" must necessarily be nearer the dwelling than it would be where the climate is fair most of the year. Ordinarily, the ideal location would be apart from the other buildings, but near enough to the barnyard, if the birds are to have free range, that they may spend part of their time there scratching. The soil about the house should be well drained. If there is no natural elevation this can be accomplished by the use of a plow and scraper, producing a gentle slope from all sides and preventing water from standing during rainy weather. A few inches of sand or gravel on the surface is helpful in the drainage. Trees planted on the north or northwest side, especially evergreens, will be useful for protection against the wind in the colder parts of the country. Winds and draughts dissipate heat generated in the body of each fowl, hence it is necessary to guard them.

The Principle of Housing—Many types of poultry houses are recommended, but all embody practically the same principle of providing shelter and fresh air. There are the so-called fresh air, open front, and semi-convertible open front houses, and modifications of the three. All have their advantages.

The Cornish fowl does not require any different housing from other breeds. Houses that successfully care for other heavy breeds, as the Orpingtons or Rocks, will do as well for Cornish. Comfortable housing is important because, on account of their weight and size, Cornish require more space per individual.

A successful house may be of the shed roof variety, 12 feet wide, or not wider than 16 feet. and any length. The size depends upon the number of birds one intends to raise annually; allowing four or more feet for each bird. The southern side should be of the semi-convertible open front type, especially in the colder climates. This type of front in case of severe cold or stormy weather, can be quickly closed by placing glass windows in the openings to take the place of the curtain which should be in place at other times.

The open front type of house has been most valuable to breeders in maintaining the health and vigor of the flock, and especially in exterminating the filth disease of poultry—roup. This open front type of house has become almost universal with breeders of poultry on account of its salubrious effect on the stock, making them sturdy and capable of withstanding variations in the weather. As a result, birds for successive generations are seldom sick.

The Material and Fixtures Used—The materials used in the construction of poultry houses is optional. Cement is good, especially for floors, making the house rodent-proof; it is sanitary and easy to keep that way. Cheap lumber, plaster board and building paper painted with coal tar make a serviceable building. Measures must always be taken to prevent draughts.

The fixtures inside the house should be movable. The reason is apparent. Houses need to be cleaned frequently and thoroughly. White washing of the interior is essential to cleanliness. Therefore, the feed boxes or hampers, nest boxes and perches should be so made that they may be completely and quickly removed.

The size and weight of the fowl must be considered when perches are made. If made of shingling lath 1x2 inches resting on trestles 18 inches apart, the upper corners smooth so as to fit the feet, and providing 10 inches for each bird, they will be admirably adapted to their purpose.

A dropping board, removable and built on trestles beneath the perches, is a necessary sanitary convience. Neither dropping board or perches should be too high from the ground. Continual jumping off a high board has a tendency to cause corns, bumble feet and accidents.

The feeding hampers and nest boxes should be arranged conveniently, and so as not to take up too much room.

Affording Ventilation—Ample ventilation is afforded by the open front of the house. In cold climates this space is covered by thin canvas or thick sheeting to prevent draughts. Some breeders suspend an additional curtain in front of the perches to retain the warmth in the perching quarters generated by the fowls and at the same time allow the circulation of fresh air.

Whether the floor is cement or wood, it is essential that it be covered with litter. This adds warmth and comfort in cold weather. It provides exercise when the fowls are enclosed, prevents disease by the absorption of moisture from the droppings, and neutralizes odors. There are various materials on the market that are especially valuable as litter. Wheat or oat straw, shredded stover, cotton-seed hulls, wheat or oat chaff, leaves, shredded cork and pine needles, any of which will serve the purpose.

Revealing the Cause of Disease—The comfort and health of Cornish is of the utmost importance, and the necessity of constructing the house in a manner conducive to these has been explained. But as careful as some breeders may be, disease sometimes infests their flocks. There are certain conditions that the often overlooked. In order to suggest a few items that may reveal a clue to the probable cause of the malady the following is given:

How Many Birds Are Sick?—The number of birds sick will give the breeder a clue as to whether the disease is infectious or is a result of some food that has disagreed with them. The age of the birds afflicted should indicate the sturdiness of the flock. If birds affected are females the probable cause may lie in the reproductive organs; the laying symptoms should be ascertained by noting the size and shape of the eggs for possible abnormality, whether there is difficulty in laying eggs, a protrusion of the vent, hemorrhage following birth of egg, or sudden death while laying. The duration of the illness is important to know.

Character of the Sickness—Examine the feathers and note the actions of birds, and whether there is fever, a loss of weight, difficult breathing or unusual sign.

Objective Symptoms—The breeder should note the condition of the head, wattles, earlobes and comb. The eyes and nose should be observed for any possible discharges and the presence of any odor. The mouth should be thoroughly examined for discharges and cankers, the latter especially in the trachea or windpipe. The condition of the legs and feet are important in determining whether they have the proper color, swellings in localized areas, or growths.

Other Considerations—The droppings should be examined to determine the color, amount, frequency and whether solid, formed or liquid. Examination should be made for lice, mites or other parasites.

Environment, Feeding—Sickness may be present on account of the lack or presence of certain housing conditions, or of faulty feeding. Notice should be taken of the amount of feed and the amount of each ingredient used. If a dry or wet mash is used, if scratch feed, green feed, grit, shells, or charcoal are used, they should be examined for possible contamination. The water should be examined.

The size and general type of the house should be considered when determining the cause or possible eradication of disease. Also the flooring should be noticed to learn if it is damp. If litter is used on the floor, it should be examined to learn if it is disease producing or whether it has become thinned out and needs changing. Notice the ventilation. Correct any evils in the fixtures which might cause an endemic disease.

Post-Mortem Examination—The importance of a post-mortem examination, that is, the opening of a fowl after death and making an examination of the condition of the internal organs, cannot be over-estimated. Frequently the symptoms shown before death are either very slight or of such a confusing nature as to make an intelligent diagnosis difficult, whereas a post-mortem examination will quickly show the cause of death.

To make the post-mortem examination the following method may be used. Lay the dead fowl breast uppermost on a table, board or top of a barrel. Spread the legs and wings and drive a small wire nail through each foot and the joint of each wing. Pluck the feathers from the breast and then cut the skin. Drawing back the skin on both sides so as to leave the flesh of the breast exposed, take a sharp knife and cut through the breast muscles on both sides of the breast bone, then using a small pair of shears or strong blunt scissors, cut out the center of the breast bone, taking care not to cut or injure the heart or other internal organs that lie just beneath. If these are injured it may cause a flow of blood that will make further observations difficult When this is done the other organs will all be seen clearly exposed and in their normal position.

The first organ you see will be the liver. In a healthy state it should be rich chocolate brown in color, free from any spots or discolorations. It should also be of a uniform firm texture and not spongy or rotten. The heart should be of a uniform texture as the liver with no undue amount of fat and evenly lobed; in other words, it should not be bulged out on one side or the other. If it is and the bird died suddenly you may rest assured the trouble was heart failure. In back of the heart and on either side lying up close to the spinal column will be seen the pink, spongy lungs. The lungs of a healthy bird will float in water. If they sink it is a good sign that they are diseased. The intestines should have no inflamed walls when examined. Notice should be made of any spots, growths or tubercles either on the intestinal walls or the investments. The contents should be examined. The egg producing organs should be inspected to ascertain the presence of a broken or misformed egg, or whether it has been punctured, allwing the egg substance to escape into the abdominal cavity. Other organs should be examined such as the kidney and spleen and pancreas for any pathological condition. Also the crop, gullet and wind-pipe should be noted for discolored spots and cankers. In cases of sudden death, fits or death which is preceded by convulsions or unusual actions, it should necessitate the removal of the top of the skull to examine the brain for growths or hemorrhages.

The Result of Unsanitary Conditions—The various afflictions of poultry are usually a result of unsanitary conditions, damp floors and lack of sunshine. By eliminating these causes disease may be prevented. Most of the diseases are filth diseases.

Should disase afflict one or more birds they should be isolated, to prevent contagion. If there are discharges or open sores they should be rendered as clean as possible and an antiseptic dusting powder used to inhibit bacterial growth. If the bowels are apparently affected, an eliminant as castor oil is valuable. If a canker impedes the breathing to any extent an attempt should be made to rupture the canker. It should be remembered that when a bird is ill it does not require food. If the bird can be filled with water by inserting a small tube about an eighth of an inch in diameter into the crop two or three times a day, it will survive many others that are not helped in this way.

Filth always means disease; guard against it.

CHAPTER X

TRAINING AND CONDITIONING FOR EXHIBITION

The Methods Used by Professionals—For one who intends to exhibit birds at a poultry show, it is essential that the methods used by the professional breeder be given consideration. He should realize in the beginning that the conditioning and training of Cornish are as important as breeding the fowl. The health, traveling stamina and behavior in the judge's hands must be ascertained and improved to the highest pitch before the exhibition takes place.

Prize winning fowls at most of the poultry shows to-day are noticeably marked by their physical condition and showroom behavior. They have been conditioned and trained a month or six weeks before they appear in public with but few exceptions. Their plumage and characteristic markings have been made to stand out prominently by previous grooming. The person who passes judgment on the birds thus prepared is necessarily influenced favorably.

Birds of exceptional type and markings are sometimes denied their rightful claim to an award, because an owner has not taken the time or trouble to make a good impression. The famous Cornish hen, "Twentieth Century Model," which won so many blue ribbons and which created such a furor on account of her type and markings, was groomed intelligently by her owners for the showroom. She was in the best physical condition possible and this was maintained during strenuous tours to the larger poultry exhibits. It cannot be too urgently impressed on the reader's mind that this phase of poultry exhibiting must be given minute attention.

"Show Game" Hints—We find many breeders of Cornish successful in every way except winning prizes at leading shows. They may have shown a few birds, and because they did not happen to win any of the prizes, they lost interest and never exhibited again. Perhaps the following suggestions will renew interest in the "show game."

The time required to spend on birds that are intended to be shown is from four to six weeks. Of course the birds that are selected must approach the Standard of Perfection as far as possible. The number chosen should be in excess of those that are to be entered in order to have a surplus of birds in case of accident or death of any of the birds. Then, too, not all birds respond to the conditioning and training methods that are employed.

It is quite necessary that coops be used and each bird handled both inside and out. This should be done carefully and skillfully. A good way is to pick the bird up by the base of the wing. This prevent breaking feathers or loosening them from the tail.. If the bird is handled as the judge would handle it, day by day, it soon learns to know what is to be expected, and a mere touch of a judge's stick will command the proper pose and carriage. Many birds have become so tame by this sort of handling

AN IMPORTED PEN

This pen from England formed part of the foundation of the COOLKENNY strain of Dark Cornish. It has won many prizes at leading American shows.

that they have won over superior birds by assuming poses that cover up defects because their owners had trained them. Birds that are to be entered in groups should be put in a pen about ten days before the exhibition, so that they will become accustomed to one another and not fight.

Grooming the Birds—Birds must be washed frequently with soap and lukewarm water, which in itself is sufficient to tame the wildest creature, and will free them from vermin. Washing improves the texture of feathers and brightens the plumage. The face, comb, wattles and legs need to be washed with water only. Unless the bright red comb and wattles of Cornish are off-color, nothing should be placed on them to attempt to check redundant growth, such as alcohol, or turpentine and cocoanut oil. These only precipitate the normal skin oil and place an artificial finish on them. Cocoanut oil or olive oil will sofen the skin, but unless this is necessary they should not ordinarily be used.

After the birds have been confined to their coop a few days they will begin to take on weight. The following regimen is followed: The first day no food is given. On account of the strangeness of the surroundings the birds do not eat. Water may be supplied. On the second day, preferably in the morning, a mixture of grit, shells, charcoal and corn is given. Fresh water

AN EGG PRODUCER

Unretouched Photo.

This hen, a prize winner at many shows, as well as being a veritable egg-machine. Trained and always kept in the best condition.

is given. The next two feedings during the day should be red wheat and Canadian flint corn. Oat sprouts may also be sparingly given. This procedure is followed for the next four or five days.

Feeding the Birds—If the conditioner believes in a variety of different foods, a mixture of cracked corn and crushed oats in equal parts make a good dry mash, with whole red wheat. Granulated beef scraps of standard brands may be given sparingly, preferably twice a week. Green feeds, as mangled wurzels, cabbage and sprouted oats are valuable. Milk, sweet or sour, and also buttermilk, which is considered the best of all, are given.

Milk contains all the essential elements of a perfect food combined with the mineral constituents that make for bone formation
and glossy plumage. Drinking troughs should be filled with this
twice a day.

Drugs that are sold on the market as tonics and system
builders are worthless and a waste of money. Proper food is al-

FROM THE SHOW ROOM

This cockerel won on account of the training and conditioning before the competition.

ways the best tonic, and we may leave to the kindly offices of
nature the work of restoring depleted fowls.

Frequent feedings will work wonders in fowls that need to
be brought up to standard weight. Three heavy meals and two
light ones should be given. The night feed should consist of as
much whole wheat and cracked corn as can be eaten in half an
hour.

Daily Feeding Schedule—The following daily schedule of
feeding as above directed may be more easily comprehended:

First Day—No food at all. Plenty of fresh water.

Second Day—Mixture of grit, shells, charcoal and cracked
corn. Second or third feeding should consist of red wheat and
Canadian flint corn. Oat sprouts sparingly given. Fresh water.

Third, Fourth and Fifth Days—The same as the second,
modified only by a good dry mash on the fifth day.

Sixth Day and Those Following—Mash made up of the following ingredients once a day, preferably in the morning:

> Ground milk crackers, four parts.
> Oatmeal, seven parts.
> Hominy, ten parts.
> Ground meat, two parts. (Meat should be partly boiled.)
> Mix thoroughly, then add
> Whole flaxseed, one tablespoonful for each bird.
> Milk, quantity sufficient to moisten mash

Daily Regimen After Sixth Day—:
Morning—
> Mash.

Middle of forenoon:
Any of the following green feeds—
> Sprouted oats.
> Lettuce.
> Mangled wurzels.

Noon:
Mash consisting of—
> Ground milk crackers.
> Milk, sweet, sour or buttermilk.

Middle of afternoon:
> Any of the green foods.
> Handful of grit.

Evening:
As much as can be eaten of—
> Red wheat.
> Canadian flint corn.
> Fresh water at all times.

Before the Show—After having decided on the birds to be
entered into competition, extra effort should be made to put them
in the best condition from the cosmetic point of view. About a
week before the show wash the birds. Use soft water if possible.
By using three buckets with wide mouths the cleansing process

may be started by filling the first with lukewarm water four inches deep. In this tub the coarse dirt is removed by the use of a small hand brush. Wet the bird so that the feathers in all sections are soaked and then use soap. Rub with the plumage, beginning with the head and hackle, then the back, tail fluff and body. When the bird has been thoroughly washed the water

A NOTABLE WINNER

Almost a perfect specimen. Perhaps no bird has received such universal praise. A winner wherever shown. Notice the lacing. A Templeton product.

should be squeezed out of the feathers as much as possible. The bird is then placed into the second tub of water which should also be lukewarm water, five or six inches deep. Rinse the bird thoroughly by use of sponge, separating feathers with the free hand. Use a second bucket of water in case the water gets too soiled or soapy.

If the bird is of a light color, either White Cornish, White Laced Red or Buff, a third bucket of water is necessary to bleach the feathers with bluing water. The strength of the bluing should be a bit stronger than that used for washing clothes. The bird is placed in the water and all parts made wet. Then all the water is removed from the plumage and the bird is taken from the water and allowed to drain off by standing on a box or barrel which is clean. Again try to get out the water in the plumage with a sponge and then dry by the use of a fan. Place the bird in a warm room or near a stove to dry. If the place is too warm it will cause the feathers to curl.

When the bird is thoroughly dried, an orange-wood stick should be used to cleanse the leg scales and toes, followed up later with a solution of sweet oil and alcohol, half and half, to give a certain polish. While in the show room before the judging takes place, the sweet oil mixture may be used on the face and wattles and comb.

With the Dark Cornish it is necessary to use judgment in the removal of an off-color or white feather. It is legitimate when it does not detract from the general appearance of the bird. Dead feathers or small ones should certainly be removed.

Every legitimate means should be used when training and conditioning birds for the showroom. Directions and rules as defined in the American Standard of Perfection concerning the competition of poultry should be kept in mind.

CHAPTER XI

JUDGING CORNISH

Score Card vs. Comparison

Facts Essential to a Novice—For the benefit of those who have never exhibited their birds and do not know just how they are handled by a poultry judge, a few instructions and explanations may be given.

For the novice, and the breeder who has never competed in the show room, it is sufficient to say that two methods of judging are practiced: (1) score card, and (2) comparison judging. Of the two, the latter is the more popular. The reason for this is quite apparent. In cases of a tie between birds that have the same score in number of points, the person judging the tied birds must in the final analysis compare the birds.

Score card judging cannot be practiced when there are a great number of birds in competition. But this is no reason why it should not be practiced in a small way by the breeder himself, or, when there are only a few birds in competition and the judge has plenty of time. On the score card every section of the bird is listed, followed by the number of points allotted each section of a perfect bird. The specimen is judged first as a whole for symmetry, after which each individual section is examined for shape and color. Whatever per cent. the judge thinks a section lacks in being perfect is deducted from a valuation of that section and the amount of the deduction or "cut" is written on the score card. The total number gives the score of the fowl.

Helpful to Small Breeder—The small breeder should score up his birds occasionally. This practice enables him to know in which sections his birds are imperfect. He should also attend poultry shows and note the prize winners, score them on his own account and note their points of perfection.

The following is the official score card of the A. P. A. It is printed on cardboard, 3½x6½ inches, and may be obtained from the Secretary of the American Poultry Association:

(Name of Association here)

(Date, month, day and year show is held here)

Official Score Card of the American Poultry Association

Exhibitor

Variety .... Sex ....

Entry No. .... Band No. .. .. Weight............

	Shape	Color
Symmetry		
Weight or Size		
Condition		
Comb		
Head		
Beak		
Eyes		
Wattles and Earlobes		
Neck		
Wings		
Back		
Tail		
Breast		
Body and Fluff		
Legs and Toes		
*Crest and Beard		
**Shortness of Feather		
Total Cuts		Score

.... Judge.

.... Secretary.

*—Applies to Crested Breeds.
**—Applies to Games and Game Bantams.

How Birds Are Judged—The bird that is judged by score card is first viewed as a whole with no consideration of its parts. It is judged according to the Standard requirements as to color and form, and whether it is true to type. The general outline is observed; the contour of the body is subjected to scrutiny. Under **symmetry**, the neck, the body, the tail and wings are especial viewed to determine their relationship to one another. The experienced judge is able to place points or " cuts " at a glance. If there is any glaring defect in the make-up of the bird it generally appears under the heading of symmetry. The faults may be found tabulated in the American Standard of Perfection with the valuation of each. These must be known thoroughly by the judge. Care must be exercised in cutting a bird for symmetry because a defect may come under a certain section; therefore " cutting " may take place a second time.

The **weight** of Cornish should be borne in mind because any bird found to be two or more pounds under weight is disqualified by the judge. Birds not up to Standard weights do not represent the breed or variety. Any that are a fraction of a pound under weight may be cut by some exacting judge using the score card. As a rule, however, this is not done.

JUDGING A CORNISH MALE BIRD

The Well-Trained Judge—A well-trained judge is usually acquainted with the **condition of birds,** and one that endeavors to pass judgment on Cornish must know how they are affected by disease, injuries, frost, travelling and handling in the show room. He must be able to find broken plumage, observe cleanliness, and determine whether a specimen is over or under weight, as a result of " stuffing " or starving. Scaly legs are inexcusable in the show room. This condition is readily cured. Birds afflicted with roup or any other disease of a contagious nature are removed from the exhibition.

The **head, beak, eyes, wattles and earlobes,** respectively are examined to determine their value on the score card. The head to obtain full count should be typically Cornish, of medium length and width, the crown slightly projecting over the eyes; the beak should be strong, well curved, stout where it joins the head; the eyes should be full size and bold in expression; the wattles and earlobes small and almost lacking and very fine in texture. When these parts do not correspond to the above, they are cut according to their respective merits. If the head is narrow it should be " cut " one half to one point. A long, straight beak should be " cut " one-half to one. Deformed beaks disqualify. For a missing eyeball, leaving an empty eye socket, one and one-half is deducted. If the wattles and earlobes are large or asymetric or wrinkled, a cut of one-half to one or one and one-half is made. The cuts on color are determined according to the variety.

The Standard allows eight points for the **comb,** but only three points should be given, as it is a small pea comb in Cornish, firm and closely set upon the head. Sometimes, as occurs in crossing, the comb is what is called a walnut comb. Mixture between a straight and pea comb termed " dubbed " comb disqualifies. The redundant comb on Cornish is cut one-half to one point according to degree. Injured or frost-bitten combs are cut one-half to one point.

The **neck** section should be of medium length and slightly arched, tapering nicely to the head, with hackle moderately short and covering base of neck   The cuts for shape are explained under " Disqualifications and Shape," and the color defects are determined according to the variety.

The **back** is an important section credited with nine points. The top line of the back is slightly convex, sloping downward from the base of the neck to the tail, and slightly sloping from each side of the spine. It is broad across the shoulders, and well filled in at the base of the neck, carrying its width well back to the juncture of the thighs and then narrowing to the tail. Size and type have much to do in giving credit to the back, and any points that are deduced depend on the dimensions of each aspect of the back. If it is too narrow, too short, too long or flat one-half to two and one-half are deducted.   Should   the saddle plumage be broken or sparsely filled, causing a decided break at the junction with the tail, one to one and one-half points are cut. The roached effect does not discredit Cornish, as the cushion of flesh follows the width between the wings. The saddle must not be dished. The saddle feathers are few in number, short and very tight fitting. Color defects depend on the variety.

Nine points for the shape and color of the **breast** makes this section an important one. The breast should be wide, deep and project slightly beyond the wing fronts when the bird stands erect. The feathers are short, and tucked between the wings at the sides. A full "crop" does not mean a full breast. A top

FROM THE REAR

Viewed from this angle the enormous shoulders may be seen and also the breadth between the legs.

view of the shoulders, wings and back should be bullock-heart shape. Cuts of one-half to two and one-half are allowed for defects in this department.

The **body and fluff** are as follows—The body in profile should resemble the outline of an egg. The large end forward and upward, with the front of keel nearly on a level with the angle at junction of back and tail. The stern is well tucked up. The feathers are scanty, short and tight-fitting. The fluff or under-color is dark slate, but may be tinged with reddish brown. In the case of an asymmetric bird with crooked breast-bone or keel bone, a cut of one and one-half to two and one-half points is allowed.

The wings are valued at seven points. Shape defects may occur frequently because there may be some variation in the powerful, closely folded wings. The wing-fronts should stand out prominently from the body at the shoulder. Broken or missing flight feathers in Dark, White and White Laced Red Cornish should be cut one and one-half points each. In the Buff Cornish they should be deducted one-half point.

Feathers or down on the shanks or toes disqualify. Knock-knees or bow-legs, an indication of weakness, should be cut to two and one-half points, also scaly legs according to the extent of the defect.

The color defects for Dark Cornish are judged according to the degree in which they deviate from the Standard. Faulty Cornish do not always lose on account of coloring: there is some glaring defect as a rule in the type of the bird, which decreases the score. A thorough knowledge of the color of Cornish, especially the Dark and White Laced Reds is necessary because of the lacing or penciling. The exhibitor should study the Standard requirements.

Important Breeding Factor—The color of eyes should always have consideration as it is a deciding factor in breeding for color. In some varieties it is sometimes thrown out of a class on account of the possible chance of reproducing defective coloring in the offspring.

Any color other than white in White Cornish disqualifies, as will any other color than rich yellow shanks and toes, including any with feathers or down on the shanks or toes. A common defect in this variety is creaminess and brassiness in the plumage. The former is caused by the presence of oil in the feathers, which is used up as the feathers mature. When found to any extent, one to one and one-half points should be deducted from each section. Brassiness is found occasionally on the surface and should be cut one to two points in each section. "Ticking," cuts one-half to two points according to the extent of the defect in each section.

Buff Cornish are disqualified when any other color but white or whitish-pink appears in the beak, shanks or toes. The plumage throughout the body should be an even shade of rich golden buff, free from shafting or mealiness. Mealiness is cut one to one and one-half in each section where found. Shafting also is cut similarly. A lemon or cinnamon buff are extremes in color. Different shades in two or more sections are serious defects   Different shades of buff cut one-half to two and one-half points. Black or white cuts from one-half to the color limit in each section.

Comparison judging lays more emphasis on typical shape with coloring second in consideration. Judging the bird as a whole is more satisfying and time saving, because the shape and coloring are taken into acount, and the final score is the same when many birds are to be judged. More time can also be spent on the good birds. Type and Cornish mean about the same to breeders. Unless Cornish possess the essential breed characteristics, they cannot be awarded first prizes, even though there is no competition in the show room. The Standard states that, "Under the comparison system, judges must deduct the full valuation of the cuts in all sections, where a specified cut is made under the heading of 'Cutting for Defects'" also "In awarding prizes by comparison, judges must consider carefully each and every section of the specimen according to the scale of points, and not allow color alone, or any one or two sections to influence their decision."

The Following Score for Comparison Judging Is of Value:

Shape, including symmetry, condition, tail and wings . .40%
Color, including tail and wings. 20%
Under-color . ... - - - 10%
Head and furnishings 10%
Legs and toes, including hardness of feather and compactness of bone 10%

The following splendid quotation from an article by F. L. Platt, Editor of the American Poultry Journal on "How to Judge by Score Card and Comparison," is given:

"Comparison judging will continue to be based on the characteristics, both shape and color, that distinguish the type. Since the comparison method will continue to be employed at the leading shows, my advice to the new exhibitor and judge is to study the characteristics of the different breeds and varieties they breed or judge, and by and by it will be said. "He knows the breed." This will mean a closer study, a fuller knowledge of the birds; it will mean judgment based on acquaintance with breed, variety and characteristics."

J. H. Drevenstedt, one of the country's most popular judges, states in an article in the American Poultry Journal, entitled "Poultry Show Judging of To-Day":

"... comparison judging was officially recognized by the American Poultry Association in 1903, and incorporated with separate instructions for judging by comparison in the American Standard of Perfection of 1905. It has come to stay...."

CHAPTER XII

THE UTILITY VALUES OF CORNISH
Crossing

What Cornish Type Has Done—While mating and rearing Cornish may be followed as an avocation only, it also has a utilitarian aspect.

That the Cornish type has stamped itself upon the minds of poultrymen is conceded. It also has brought about a certain change in the production of market fowl. It has been used for crossing on other breeds in order to increase carcass size.

Egg records have been kept of Cornish layers and it has been found that as a general rule, the breed lays as many if not more eggs than some of the so-called dual purpose fowls. Within the poultry fraternity there has been a constant effort to solve the problem of weight and egg production on the same frame. But Cornish enthusiasts demand a fair average egg production from the breed as a whole instead of an occasional individual bird with a high egg yield record.

To forsake the established Cornish type for egg production would be a false move and possibly ruin the breed entirely. Yet to modify slightly certain individuals possessing a low egg yield could not greatly harm the breed, and would increase its popularity with those who now believe it to be unprolific or unable to even reproduce itself. This can be done. It has been shown that the English sparrow has been induced to lay as high as 51 eggs in a breeding season, and pheasants from 100 to 110 eggs in the same time. The inference is plain. With a trifle attention to breaking up the periods of broodiness which often upsets the egg laying season, and by lengthening and making more full the tucked-up stern of so many poor layers, Cornish will be no longer " strictly a fancier's fowl."

Efficiency Without Trapnesting—A good and efficient method, which does away with the time consuming trapnesting, to determine which of the hens are doing the laying, is to examine each bird in the morning by feeling for the presence of an egg in the oviduct. If there is an egg present it will be found tucked up and backward against the spine. It cannot be confused with the gizzard, which lies low in the abdomen. When each bird has been recorded no further notice need be kept of the nests. It will be found this test will prove true 97 times out of 100.

The varieties having an infusion of Leghorn or Wyandotte blood will naturally be prolific layers. Their frames are constructed on the lines for egg production. The Dark variety should therefore be given some consideration if a change in the tucked-up effect is to be made.

. **The Result of Egg Laying Contests**—Egg laying contests have helped the Cornish enthusiasts to produce records which can hardly be outdone: "The Philadelphia North American," conducted at Storrs, Conn., two contests in 1913-14. J. W. Ward, Jr., in the 1914 A. C. C. Annual Year Book, in an article entitled "Cornish a Utility Fowl as well as a Fancier's Fowl," wrote as

WHY CORNISH ARE POPULAR!

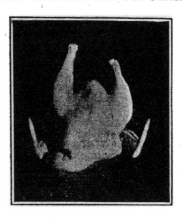

"Cornish on every farm" is a slogan which is being recognized by the farmers. Birds like this do not have to be caponized to make weight.

follows; " .....comparing the results of the first 26 weeks of each contest, or down to date, which includes the winter period from January to June—the two great periods of every poultryman's calendar, I noticed with pride that the pen of Dark Cornish in the first contest had an average of 6.3 eggs each during the above all-important period, had actually beaten out by a large margin, in almost every case, the Silver Wyandottes, the Golden Wyandottes, the S. C. Buff Leghorns, Anconas, egg-laying breeds; the S. C. Black Minorcas, the Houdans, and the much-touted Buttercups, and came within an average of 5 eggs per hen, in some cases less for the period, of tying all the Rocks, four varieties, actually beating the Wyandottes, 5 varieties, came within an average of 5 of the Langshans and all the Leghorns, an egg-laying breed with 35 pens in the contest.

"In the second contest, Cornish have also done well, being represented by the pen of White Laced Red Cornish. They have beaten out the Black Orpingtons and the Buttercups to date. They laid 281 eggs from Feb. 7, 1913, to May 30, 1913. One week they laid 30 eggs; one pullet has laid 7 eggs for a week several times.

"In short, these birds have averaged 56 eggs since they have been in the contest, and at that were greatly handicapped by being hatched very late with the exception of one bird."

The Earning Power of Birds—In the production of eggs, Cornish average about two eggs for each pound of feed consumed. In one year, each hen averages about 150 eggs to 75 pounds of feed. Ninety eggs is estimated to pay for feed and maintenance and the hen that lays even 100 eggs is 10 eggs profit.

It has been found that White Cornish average 156 eggs per year; White Laced Red and Buff Cornish average about 140 to 150 eggs per year; and Dark Cornish about 110 to 133 eggs per year. It has been found also that some strains of Cornish go broody from one to four times a year and those birds usually have the highest egg averages Males in pens reduce the egg yield in a year Color has little or no influence on the egg yield; but a large red comb indicates health and possible high egg production Two-thirds of the eggs are laid in the first half of the day and year.

Obtaining Large Egg Yields—To obtain a large egg yield it is necessary to have the proper environment. Houses of the shutter front type, with windows on each side and shutter ventilator in the center are the best. The yards should be 30x120 feet. Wheat for the fall of the year and winter green food and oats for the spring, should not be counted in the feed rations.

The feed required for egg-laying Cornish is important. The feed is composed of both grain and mash, that is, two parts grain to one part mash. This is made up as follows:

Grain feed, equal parts of cracked corn and whole wheat.

For mash, equal parts of ground oats, wheat bran, shorts or middlings, corn meal and beef scraps. Added to this is one pound of table salt to each one hundred pounds of mash. During the heavy laying season five pounds of bone meal are added to the hundred pounds of mash. During the moulting season, five pounds of O. P. oil meal should be added to the mash. Grit, oyster shells and water should be before the layers all the time. The use of feed hoppers is valuable in large plants where labor has to be considered.

The Meat Qualities—Very little need be said about the meat producing qualities of Cornish. The frames are so built that the flesh is evenly distributed. The back, the breast, the wings and legs are very muscular, making the fowl ideal for market. The front view of a dressed carcass shows the full-fleshed, well-rounded breast, and from the back it is seen immediately that there is more meat than on any other breed, unless special crate fattening or artificial cramming is resorted to. In this latter case a distasteful fat is produced which detracts from the flavor.'

The carcass of Cornish, either pure or crossed, is to be found on the markets in England to the extent of "73 per cent." of any other breeds. In this country Cornish crosses are rapidly gain-ing favor. Because of the potency of the Cornish male and its ability to stamp its progeny with its own type, it is being used extensively by farmers on mongrel stock.

For many years the Dorking-Cornish crosses have led all competitors in the "Carcass classes' at the shows in England.

MEAT QUALITIES

The muscular development of this breed is startling. For crossing purposes it cannot be excelled. This bird is a heavy weight winner.

In this country many breeders catering to fancy market trade invariably use Cornish on account of its finely fibered meat with small amount of offal.

Breeds That " Nick " Well—Not all crosses make the best

table fowl. It is well to name the breeds that " nick " best with Cornish. Dark Cornish on Dark Dorkings make an ideal cross; Dark Cornish on Golden Wyandottes; White Cornish on White Plymouth Rocks. The Cornish-Orpington cross is a favorite to bring out birds for caponizing. Crossing with Barred Rocks produces black females; Wyandottes revert to either a solid black or white Wyandotte; the females usually being black. The cross with Rhode Island Red produces a beautifully colored female and black stippled male. The Leghorn-Cornish cross matures quickly, averaging 8 pounds in 6 months.

The only motive in crossing two different breeds is to produce a specialty meat fowl, such as a capon or a soft roaster. In making any cross it should not be promiscuous. Care should be taken to study the ancestral make-up of both breeds.

Making Capons—Many persons have not recognized the simplicity of the operation upon cockerels for making capons. With a set of instruments, which can be purchased at any poultry supply house, and a little practice, anyone can master the technic. Caponizing cockerels produces some of the finest grades of poultry carcasses.

There are two profits to be derived from capons. The first. or indirect one, is greater egg production from pullets, and stronger pullets as a result of the absence of males, and second, or direct, the realization of an average of twice as much weight as the uncaponized rooster.

Capons grow fast. They dress up to standard market requirements within a very short time. In the time that it takes to put plumage on the looser feathered breeds, an extra pound of meat can be gained, especially with Cornish. It is said that the more rapid the growth, the more tender is the meat. It is not unusual to have capons that weigh 12 to 13 pounds in the course of 7 to 8 months

The hotels and restaurants buy Cornish capons because they are able to feed a larger number of persons. Cornish capons are becoming a rival to the national bird, the turkey.

The Result of Incompetent Methods—Many promising Cornish get a poor start on account of incompetent methods in hatching and rearing, to say nothing of faulty judgment used in mating. Allow them to be incubated and brooded rightly, allow them to have the proper feed and regular hours for feeding, give them free range, open air and sunshine, and the great general purpose fowl—Cornish—will thrive. Birds hatched and reared in small bare runs, especially after the first or second generations are never strong, nor are they heavy layers. The cause is apparent. If small ranged birds cannot work off the food ingested, they get lazy, their appetites diminish and the result is that the egg basket remains empty. Vim, vigor and vitality are essential for egg yielding Cornish.

Those who supply the market with Cornish carcasses must use certain methods to attain success. Good flesh producing food must be supplied at all times to make the birds grow without a setback. When the time comes to market them, according to requirements, it will be found most profitable not to feed them for at least 24 hours before.

Preparing For the Market—The bird is killed by running a sharply pointed knife through the roof of the mouth producing a

THE AMERICAN CORNISH CLUB EMBLEM

large open wound from which the blood may flow freely. By hanging the bird up by the feet the blood is allowed to drain from the body. The legs are picked of feathers without wetting them. The carcass is held by the head and legs and dipped into hot water just below the boiling point, three or four times. Keeping the head out of the hot water prevents the discoloration of the comb and wattles, sinking in of the eyes and giving the head an otherwise unhealthy appearance. The feathers are picked immediately, including pin-feathers. Care should be taken not to rupture the skin as it gives it a blotchy effect. To complete the operation the carcass is "plumped" by placing the body of the carcass into clean hot water and then immediately into cold water. It is then hung up and allowed to drain and become perfectly cold before packing.

To make a neat appearing box of Cornish carcasses, the head should be slipped under the wing, the legs straightened out and the birds placed side by side in a box which holds 12. This prevents any slipping in the box during transit.

Shipping Birds For Breeding—When shipping birds to individuals for breeding purposes, or to live poultry markets, it is wise to use crates which are durable, comfortable and sanitary. The practice of using cardboard boxes or under-sized wooden boxes is to be condemned.

By using a deep crate, which may be obtained from local supply houses, or manufactured specially, plenty of breathing space is obtained. A piece of muslin over the top with slats nailed over it will prevent the bird from getting its head out, and at the same time, allow a free supply of air. Holes in the sides also help in case anything is piled on top of the box.

THE END.

CONTENTS

CPSIA information can be obtained
at www.ICGtesting.com
Printed in the USA
BVHW041819070319
542065BV00006B/120/P